T0303891

GARLAND STUDIES ON

INDUSTRIAL PRODUCTIVITY

edited by

STUART BRUCHEY
UNIVERSITY OF MAINE

INDUSTRIAL INEFFICIENCY AND DOWNSIZING

A STUDY OF LAYOFFS AND PLANT CLOSURES

MATTHEW B. KREPPS
AMY BERTIN CANDELL

Routledge
Taylor & Francis Group

NEW YORK AND LONDON

First published by Garland Publishing, Inc.

This edition by Routledge:

Routledge
Taylor & Francis Group
2 Park Square, Milton Park
Abingdon, Oxon OX14 4RN

Routledge
Taylor & Francis Group
711 Third Avenue
New York, NY 10017

Much of Chapter 2 is reprinted from an article by Richard E.
Caves and Matthew B. Krepps in *Brookings Papers on Economic
Activity Microeconomics 2: 1993*, pp. 227–288, with the kind
permission of The Brookings Institution, Washington, D.C.

Library of Congress Cataloging-in-Publication Data

Krepps, Matthew B., 1969–
    Industrial inefficiency and downsizing : a study of layoffs and
plant closures / Matthew B. Krepps and Amy Bertin Candell.
        p.   cm. — (Garland studies on industrial productivity)
    Includes bibliographical references and index.
    ISBN 0-8153-3017-0 (alk. paper)
    1. Plant shutdowns—United States. 2. Downsizing of organi-
zations—United States. 3. Industrial efficiency—United States.
4. Organizational effectiveness—United States. I. Candell, Amy
Bertin. II. Title. III. Series.
HD5708.55.U6K74   1997
338.6'042—dc21

                                                    97-25278

Contents

v

List of Tables and Figures

Preface

This book is, in a proximate sense, a product of our recently completed doctoral dissertations in economics at Harvard University. Ultimately it results from the interest we both have in industrial organization and the study of markets. This interest, nurtured most directly by our common thesis advisor, Richard E. Caves, explains the common links, both thematic and methodological, among the chapters contained herein.

The primary focus of the book is an inquiry into the behavior of firms in response to competitive forces. The studies in this book investigate the genesis and exodus of industrial inefficiency by analyzing where corporate fat accumulates and how it is eliminated in response to competitive forces. In the long run, severe increases in competitive pressure are generally presumed to force inefficient producers to reach the production frontier or exit the industry. Consistent with this common perception, we find that increases in industry-level import competition, merger activity, and declines in industry demand explain a large fraction of layoffs and plant closures by firms or plants that are subject to inefficiency. The implementation of downsizing in response to these competitive pressures, however, is often undertaken in a seemingly suboptimal fashion. Managers preannounce layoffs in spite of their convictions that such behavior undermines employee morale and productivity. Further, managers close plants that are not among the most inefficient in the industry. We find that these puzzling managerial actions, though ostensibly inefficient, are perfectly consistent with profit-maximizing behavior if one adopts the perspective of the firm as a whole. This seemingly unproductive behavior can be reconciled by recognizing that although productivity measures are typically static plant-level measures, managers are optimizing the dynamic value of the firm.

In addition to the thematic links about productivity, the chapters in this book are linked by an approach to modeling. The framework in each chapter explicitly recognizes that firms and plants differ in measurable ways, and that outside demand shocks can be used to illuminate strategic interactions and supply relationships across firms or plants within industries. By modeling firm and plant responses to outside shocks through the lens of corporate optimization, we hope to cast new light on output and employment decisions and the plant closure decision.

We have had considerable help and support in making this book a reality. The research that underlies this book would never have been completed without the unflagging guidance of Richard Caves, who was both teacher and mentor to both of us since early in our academic lives. We would also like to thank the other members our thesis committees for the time, energy, and intelligence they applied in helping us to complete our dissertations. George Baker, Ken Corts, Tim Bresnahan, Dan Raff and Michael Whinston cheerfully endured numerous drafts of these papers and did much to help us improve them.

We received useful comments from seminar participants at Harvard University, Harvard Business School, the National Bureau of Economic Research, the Federal Reserve Board of Governors, University of Michigan Business School, University of Nevada-Reno, Columbia Business School, New York University, Kellogg School of Management, INSEAD, Emory University, and Arizona State University. In addition we would like to thank the following colleagues for useful comments and discussions: Margaret Blair, Larry Candell, Pankaj Ghemawat, Adam Jaffe, Joseph Kalt, Steve Kaplan, Karen Model, Bruce Petersen, David Reishus, Joanna Stavins, and Frank Wolak.

Richard Caves co-authored the paper reproduced in large part as Chapter 2 of this book. Without implicating him in the production of this book, it would not have come into existence without his insights and knowledge of the field. We also thank The Brookings Institution for generously allowing us to reprint the original version of our paper that appeared in the 1992 Microeconomics volume of *The Brookings Papers on Economic Activity*.

The Depression-era Census of Manufacturers manuscripts utilized in Chapter 4 came from Tim Bresnahan and Dan Raff. The Harvard Business School and the National Science Foundation provided financial support for the laborious process of creating a machine readable database from the microfilm manuscripts.

The Harvard Business School, Division of Research contributed generous financial support to each of the chapters in this book. Chris Allen of the Harvard Business School, Division of Research was instrumental in assisting with the compilation of data. Valuable research assistance was contributed by Greg Bell, Aviv Nevo, Rolland Ho, Sung Nam, Asif Ahmad, Mina Yu, Jackie Coleman, and John Kalyvas.

Kyanna Sutton, Bridget Kane, and Sally Caraganis expertly edited the final manuscript of this book.

Industrial Inefficiency
and Downsizing

I

Introduction

The large reductions of employment in major U.S. companies during the past decade raise the question of how this apparent "fat" accumulates in corporate hierarchies and what shocks promote its removal. More generally, what forces drag firms away from the best-practice productivity frontier within their respective industries and how do the inefficient firms regain their competitiveness?

In this book we depart from the standard point-forward methodology of analyzing competitive shocks and drawing inferences about the optimality of firms' responses to those competitive disturbances. Rather, we begin by describing in detail how firms and production entities within them could have gotten to the point where a substantial reduction in the resources they employed was mandated. Having developed a theory of fat accumulation, we analyze three large-scale shocks to U.S. manufacturing that have occurred during this century: the tremendous surge in import competition that began during the late 1970s, the wave of activity in the market for corporate control that began in the early 1980s, and the Great Depression of the 1930s.

Recognizing that there are important (and measurable) differences between plants within a given firm, firms within a given industry, and industries within the manufacturing sector of the U.S. economy, we analyze both the nature and efficiency of responses to major external shocks at the plant level, the firm level, and the industry level. The questions we pose are: 1) What form did the responses to these competitive threats take, either with attempts to regain competitive superiority or to abandon inferior entities, and 2) Were the patterns of response consistent with theories of intended profit maximization? In the context of layoffs, these questions address the efficiency of implementation, while in the context of exit, these questions concern the relative efficiency of plants that were closed versus those that remained open.

Chapter 2 begins by developing a testable theory of the onset of industrial inefficiency. It is commonplace in popular discourse that large, successful corporations tend to acquire bloated staffs; many economists give credence to this behavior when they seek (and find) favorable effects on productivity of management buyouts, "refocusing" of diversified enterprises, the excision of layers of supervisory management, and other reorganizations put forth as means to improve productivity. Yet only with caution does one maintain any hypothesis about productivity shortfall or technical inefficiency, lest s/he seem ignorant of the Law of Cash-Strewn Footpaths: if cost efficiency could be improved, somebody would already have profited by improving it.

We therefore describe the mechanisms that could shield employees (particularly white-collar employees) from the reach of the profit-seeking manager. The factors we consider are the ease with which managers can measure the revenue productivity of nonproduction employees, and the ways in which business goals other than profit-maximization might affect the number of nonproduction workers recruited and retained.

We then test this theory by investigating whether nonproduction employment in U.S. manufacturing behaves as if fat could be excised by the squeezing. The investigation proceeds through two stages. First, working with disaggregated manufacturing industries observed over the period 1967-1986, we ask whether industry-level nonproduction employment was reduced by circumstances that render excess nonproduction employment no longer viable: mergers (distinguished as "related" or "conglomerate") and changes in imports' share of U.S. consumption at those times and in those sectors where one would expect it. Since these disturbances may excise fat from all of an industry's firms rather than merely reallocating activity among the industry's member firms, it is desirable to test our hypotheses at the industry level.

We then examine announcements of corporate downsizings at the firm-level from 1987-1991 to observe how the stock market reacted. The results, although qualified, are satisfyingly consistent with our theory of industrial inefficiency: by the 1980s, bursts of import competition and of changes in corporate control did significantly reduce nonproduction employment, and shareholders came to react positively to downsizings that involved white-collar layoffs and related reorganizations.

Given the apparent significance of the efficiency-impeding bureaucratic dynamics outlined in Chapter 2, we turn our attention in Chapters 3 and 4 to the question of whether and to what degree responses to external shocks can be characterized as inefficient. Chapter 3 deepens the analysis of layoff implementation begun at the end of Chapter 2 by exploring an empirical incongruity: although layoffs are ostensibly management's signal that they heard the market's wake-up call (as evinced by the evidence in Chapter 2), many layoffs are implemented in seemingly suboptimal fashion. The particular case addressed in this section of the book concerns layoffs that are announced long before they are implemented.

Extensive field research indicates that managers believe preannouncing impending layoffs adversely affects worker productivity, yet such voluntary disclosures occur. In a disproportionate share of cases, layoff announcements with long lead times immediately precede borrowing by the announcer or its rivals. This chapter tests the proposition that these preannouncements are a form of costly disclosure undertaken by managers who are unable to commit contractually to future layoffs in order to influence capital costs.

The theory we test is that although the decision to preannounce layoffs may appear suboptimal from a narrow product market perspective, preannouncement may nonetheless be profit-maximizing if the benefits that redound to the firm as a result of signals sent to the capital markets outweigh the perceived productivity losses. Our approach is similar to recent work in the industrial organization literature on the linkages between product markets and capital markets, in that we exploit the fact that product market decisions and capital market decisions are not independent. Empirical evidence presented in this section suggests that the need to obtain outside financing—by the announcer or its product market rivals—is an important determinant of these putatively costly preannouncements.

Chapter 4 sharpens the focus of the analysis to the plant level, examining the decisions about plant closure in a period of severe external shocks in order to examine linkages between plant efficiency and plant closure. During the Great Depression, blast furnace plants, a component of the steel industry, experienced a sharp downturn in demand, one that could be expected to "rationalize" the industry and force out inefficient producers. But this is not the pattern that we observed. Even after controlling for measurable differences in technology and organizational structure, the pattern of plant closure is not fully consistent with "survival of the fittest." Using a stochastic production function to measure the distance that each plant is from the frontier that defines best practice, many of the plants that closed are a similar distance from the frontier as plants that remain open.

On the surface, the plant closure decisions may appear inconsistent with cost-minimizing behavior. The results of this puzzle, however, are consistent with the conclusions of Chapter 3: the decision is viewed as suboptimal only when viewed narrowly through the lens of the plant rather than of the firm as a whole. The blast furnace plants were part of an integrated process that produces steel, and the mixture of efficient and inefficient outcomes for blast furnace plants reflects the fact that production decisions are coordinated with adjacent steel plants. Given these rigidities implied by coordination, the pattern we observe is likely an efficient outcome, though it implies substantial inefficiencies when compared to an industry-wide cost minimum under which only the most efficient plants operated.

In conclusion, the timing and incidence of downsizing and plant closure are consistent with the theory that the organizational dynamics of large, successful firms inhibit their ability to remain at the productivity frontier; however, we find no evidence of inefficiency in firms' responses to these external shocks. On the contrary, for the layoffs and plant closure decisions that we examine, the appearance of inefficient responses to competitive threats can be explained by the attribution to managers of an overly narrow optimand. When layoffs and plant closures are analyzed from the perspective of the firm as a whole, taking into account measurable differences across agents as well as the strategic interactions with competitors in capital and product markets, the downsizing behavior we observe is fully consistent with profit-maximizing and cost-minimizing behavior.

II

Fat: The Displacement of Nonproduction Workers and the Efficiency of U.S. Manufacturing Industries

2.1. INTRODUCTION

In the long run American Industry has relied increasingly on nonproduction staff, yet in the last decade many white-collar employees have been squeezed out of large corporations in the name of increased efficiency. Were exceptional shocks and competitive pressures responsible for inducing corporate weight-loss campaigns? How could administrative "fat" have accumulated in the first place?

In this paper we investigate the possibility that nonproduction employment in U.S. manufacturing behaves as if "fat" could be excised by the squeezing. The investigation proceeds through two stages. First, working with disaggregated manufacturing industries observed over 1967-1986, we ask whether industry-level nonproduction employment was reduced by circumstances that render excess nonproduction employment no longer viable: mergers (distinguished as "related" or "conglomerate") and changes in imports' share of U.S. consumption at those times and in those sectors where one would expect it. We then examine announcements of corporate downsizings during 1987-1991 to observe how the stock market reacted. The results, although qualified, are satisfyingly consistent: by the 1980s bursts of import competition and of changes in corporate control did significantly reduce nonproduction employment, and shareholders came to react positively to downsizings that involve white-collar layoffs and related reorganizations.

For a framework this analysis draws upon the hypothesis that firms—especially successful large firms—are organizational coalitions capable of employing and retaining levels of nonproduction employment in excess of what would maximize their profits. It has this implication that is central to our statistical test: unanticipated disturbances that shrink these coalitions' capacities to meet members' reservation demands force reductions in white-collar employment.[1] At most we expect to establish that this framework provides a *sufficient* explanation for some recent changes in nonproduction employment. To show *necessity* would impossibly require ruling out all plausible reasons why (for example) reduced nonproduction employment might be a value-maximizer's efficient submissive response to an upsurge of import competition.

2.2. NONPRODUCTION EMPLOYMENT IN MANUFACTURING: QUANTITATIVE PATTERNS

During the prosperous 1980s many white-collar employees discovered that the presumptively secure ground beneath their feet had become shaky. The growth of white-collar employment in large corporations was arrested, and a shift in the distribution of employment toward smaller companies caught public attention. Concern was voiced by some economists that takeovers and other changes in corporate control among large firms were occasions for breaking long-term employment contracts with workers who had suffered wages less than their marginal products in their younger days in anticipation of excess compensation in their maturity.[2] The recent recession launched an unprecedented assault on white-collar unemployment; in the year following August 1989, 65 percent of the increase in total unemployed workers were managers, professionals, and clerical workers.[3] Business gurus lauded the process, urging the breakdown of "functional silos" of bureaucratic authority and the creative use of information technologies.[4]

Changes in nonproduction employment of course depend on changes in its use as an input efficiently combined with others as well as on any changes in its excess use. The long-run trend has been upward: the proportion of nonproduction workers in total employment in U.S. manufacturing rose from 26.4 percent in 1967 to 32.1 percent in 1990. Berman, Bound, and Griliches found that this increase was due both to changes in the composition of manufacturing industries and to increased white-collar proportions in the typical four-digit industry. This upgrading of the labor-skill input continued during the 1980s input proceeded in the face of rising relative wages for nonproduction employees. In cross-section they found the complementarity of capital and skill to be statistically significant although not an important factor, and they also linked changes in nonproduction employment's share (1979-1987) to industries' rates of investment in computers, their rates of research and development activity and (less formally) to plants' usage of new technologies.[5]

We sought evidence on changes in white-collar employment patterns in the *Occupation by Industry* data of the population census, only to find 1990 data not yet available and the analysis of changes over 1970-1980 hobbled by a major change in the classification system. However, the earlier period yielded some evidence on the distribution of patterns among manufacturing industries. We concluded that for 53 two- and three-digit manufacturing industries it was possible to determine the numbers employed in 1970 and 1980 for each category of nonproduction workers shown in Table 2.1.[6] We wanted to determine how these numbers employed grew relative to one another taking real-output changes into account. We first adjusted crudely for each industry's real-output change by calculating its percentage change in each employment category and subtracting the percentage change in its real output.[7] This adjustment would be correct if the elasticity of nonproduction employment with respect to real output was unity; it is probably smaller (as our regression analysis will suggest), but the discrepancy does not distort the distribution of industries' "excess" changes for one class of nonproduction employment relative to another class. Results are shown in Table 2.1. In the median industry employment in executive, administrative, managerial, and sales occupations

Table 2.1
Distribution of increases of nonproduction employment adjusted for
increase of real output, by category of nonproduction employees, 53
manufacturing industries, 1970-1980

Type of nonproduction employment	25th percentile	median	75th percentile
Executive, administrative, managerial	36.4%	20.6%	-3.4%
Professional specialty, technical support	10.9	-10.5	-35.2
Administrative support	11.4	-1.6	-29.2
Services	14.7	-4.5	-21.8

Source: Calculated from U.S. Bureau of the Census (1972) and U.S. Bureau of
the Census (1984) (see text).

Note: Each line reports the distribution across industries of percentage increase
in the nonproduction employment category minus percentage increase in
real output. As a measure of "excess growth" of nonproduction employment this difference is biased downward, but comparisons along the columns of the table should be unbiased.

grew considerably fastest. Professional specialty and technical support
personnel—the "knowledge workers" of the white-collar cadre—grew
slowest, with administrative support staff (e.g. secretaries) and service
workers (e.g. security personnel) in between. The same differential is
evident at the 25th and 75th percentiles of the distributions. Because
the adjustment for the industry's change in real output is biased upward
and the estimated excess growth rates of employment thus biased
downward, the median industry's large excess figure for executive occupations (20.6 percent) is particularly arresting. How this increase in
the 1970s was divided between efficient new technologies of organization and squeezable "fat" is an interesting question.

In the 1980s, when losses of white-collar jobs allegedly accelerated, manufacturing employment remained about stationary after the
recovery from the 1981-1982 recession. The data presented in Table
2.2 show this both in the aggregate and for the major white-collar categories.

Table 2.2
Nonproduction-worker employment, its components, and total employment, U.S. manufacturing sector 1983-1987 (thousands)

Year		Executive	Professional	Technicians and related support	Sales	Administrative Support	Service	All
1983	D[a]	1,195	1,028	509	271	1,393	204	11,708
	ND	816	491	203	391	1,045	184	8,238
1984	D	1,370	1,083	530	307	1,494	213	12,606
	ND	836	486	209	440	1,051	173	8,389
1985	D	1,419	1,148	540	307	1,464	227	12,586
	ND	869	489	206	440	1,065	173	8,293
1986	D	1,416	1,192	567	295	1,425	210	12,605
	ND	878	510	198	425	1,060	177	8,357
1987	D	1,421	1,166	498	292	1,410	196	12,478
	ND	894	522	202	412	1,060	164	8,456

Source: U.S. Bureau of Labor Statistics, *Labor Force Statistics Derived from the Current Population Survey, 1948-87*, Bulletin No. 2307 (1988), Table B-13, pp. 655-663.

[a]D indicates durable-goods manufacturing industries, ND nondurables.

Table 2.3
Displacement rates for selected industries and occupations, 1979-83
and 1985-89 (percent)

Employee group	Years 1979-83	Years 1985-89
Total	8.3	6.4
Industry		
Mining	26.6	22.0
Construction	19.2	12.3
Manufacturing	16.7	11.4
Durable goods	18.4	12.1
Nondurable goods	14.0	10.2
Transportation and public utilities	8.8	6.7
Wholesale and retail trade	8.4	8.7
Finance, insurance, and real estate	2.9	6.6
Services	5.6	4.8
Occupation		
Executive, administrative, and managerial	5.9	5.9
Professional specialty	3.1	3.1
Technicians and related support	6.6	6.2
Sales	7.9	6.5
Administrative support, clerical	5.7	6.0
Service occupations	4.3	3.7
Precision production, craft, and repair	12.7	8.0
Operatives, fabricators, and laborers	16.9	11.3

Source: U.S. Bureau of Labor Statistics, *Displaced Workers, 1985- 1989*, Bulletin No. 2382 (1991), Table 3, p. 4.

Since 1979 the Bureau of Labor Statistics has surveyed employees displaced from jobs they had held for three or more years. In general these displacement rates (proportion of total employees in the category who lost jobs) vary as one would expect with aggregate employment. Table 2.3 compares displacement rates for the periods 1979-1983 (embracing a recession) and 1985-1989 (covering prosperous years).

Displacement rates were lower in the latter period in the aggregate and in manufacturing (although not all service sectors). Among occupation groups displacement rates are as expected lower for white- than for blue-collar workers. However, in managerial and professional specialty occupations displacements showed no decline between the two periods, and the declines for other white-collar categories were smaller than for blue-collar workers. The same conclusions follow if 1983-1987 rather than 1985-1989 is compared to 1979-1983. In the mid-1980s nonproduction workers evidently found themselves in less firmly tenured positions than before. Apparently the pattern continued into the recent recession; according to the Bureau of Labor Statistics, of the 485,000 workers added to the unemployed between August 1989 and August 1990, 34.6 percent were managers and professionals, 30.5 percent clerical, 6.4 percent sales and technical personnel, and only 18.6 percent blue-collar.[8]

Also relevant to the question of excised fat is how hard displaced employees found it to regain jobs and how much deterioration of terms of employment they accepted. Of displaced employees who were re-employed in January 1990, in the aggregate 43.2 percent reported accepting lower wages or salaries than before. In manufacturing and in transportation and public utilities these proportions were higher, 49.1 and 51 percent, respectively, and in durable-goods manufacturing they were higher still (overall 50.9 percent, 51.7 percent in nonelectrical machinery, 59.5 percent in transportation equipment). The data are consistent with either quasi-rents (to skills) or rents having been lost more commonly in manufacturing than elsewhere; the data unfortunately are not broken down by occupation.[9] Also relevant is the frequency with which employees displaced in the 1980s were re-employed in different lines of work. Although two-thirds of administrative support workers were re-employed in similar jobs, fewer than half of the executives, administrators, and managers found jobs similar to their old ones (17 percent accepted sales jobs, 14 percent administrative-support occupations).[10]

These data do not specifically tie the displacement of white-collar workers to the downsizing of large corporations, but the downsizing itself is readily shown. In 1978 48.6 percent of all workers were employed in companies with fewer than 100 workers, but in 1984 the figure had risen to 51 percent, and employment in companies with more than 1,000 workers fell from 18.6 to 16.2 percent.[11] These discharges are held to accompany the removal of layers of middle management, shortening lines of communication within large enterprises and increasing the reaction speeds of those who remain, but the linkage of displacements to such reorganizations has not been quantified.[12]

2.3. WHY NONMAXIMIZING EMPLOYMENT OF NONPRODUCTION WORKERS?

That non-maximizing behavior in large firms is necessary to explain these patterns is not a hypothesis that we maintain. It might explain some of the movements of nonproduction employment, however, depending on the mechanisms that can shield white-collar employment from the reach of the profit-seeking manager. We consider two factors: the ease with which managers can measure the revenue productivity of nonproduction employees, and the ways business goals other than profit-maximization might affect the number of nonproduction workers recruited and retained.

Measuring White-Collar Productivity

Nonproduction jobs are diverse, and some of them (such as sales representatives) generate revenue products that probably are as easily measured by managers as those of most production-worker jobs. Nonetheless, many white-collar employees engage in team production, making the output of the individual worker difficult or impossible to observe accurately. That managers grope for efficient organizational structures in the face of prevalent team production is presumed by major lines of the organizational theory of the firm.[13] Furthermore, even when outputs (whether team or individual) can be measured in physical terms (memoranda produced?), it is far from obvious that the physical product can be related to revenue productivity for the firm.

For evidence on this conjecture we turned to the literature on personnel administration. The views we found there concur that white-collar output can at best be measured in forms that are noncommensurable with revenue productivity. Caution is urged in the use of such approximate measures; typically they capture imperfectly the tasks that white-collar employees are directed to perform, and their use in incentive and reward schemes can readily distort the allocation of effort. One literature survey flatly states that there exists no broadly acceptable approach to measuring white-collar productivity. The practitioner literature has turned to finding ways to improve productivity while finessing the problem of how to measure what is being improved.[14]

It seems clear that the would-be value-maximizing manager cannot accurately make the marginal product/wage comparison needed to optimize white-collar employment. Furthermore, quantification is more elusive for the central managerial hierarchy and its support personnel than it is for specialists and service personnel whose outputs are less commingled in team production. The situation accords with economists' habit of treating the firm's managerial hierarchy as a cost that is fixed although avoidable upon shutdown, an implicit confession of ignorance as to how this cost varies with the scale and other dimensions of the firm's activities.

Managerial Behavior

If lack of information on white-collar workers' value productivity impedes the precise optimization of actual nonproduction employment, the play of managers' and employees' objectives might lead to excessive white-collar employment, as several lines of analysis suggest. Oliver Williamson's nominees for objectives in the managerial utility function included two that favor excess white-collar employment. It is directly inflated by a preference for "staff," assistants who contribute to the ease of or satisfaction derived from top-executive jobs. It is indirectly enlarged by a preference for taking decisions of large scope, because staff are presumably needed to evaluate and execute the grand designs that they involve.[15]

The inflation of white-collar employment is also a conditional prediction of what we call the Carnegie approach to the organization and behavior of the firm. That school emphasized not the objectives of the chief executive as "principal" in vertical contracts with the firm's employees but the preferences of functional specialists whose lateral contracts specify their respective contributions, responsibilities, and expected rewards, and thereby define a synthesized objective function for the firm as a whole. In the comparative statics of this model as developed by Cyert and March, an excess of revenue to the firm over the minimum demands of the coalition members represents "slack" that can be absorbed as side payments (either pecuniary or policy payoffs) as well as reported excess profits.[16] This lateral-contracts approach is notably consistent with the idea that the ongoing firm operating in an uncertain environment possesses a repertory of team-based skills that rest on tacit knowledge. Plying these skills in light of revealed opportunities and threats depends on the cooperation of disparate team members and not some chief engineer's master blueprint.[17]

That policy payoffs from slack could lead to expanded white-collar employment was argued indirectly by Niskanen.[18] The government bureaucracy was his prototype, but he remarked that the analysis applies to any component of a firm that is not a profit center but subject to budgetary financing by a central decision-maker. Not only do regular employees gain personally in various ways when their bureau expands, he argued, but indeed their advocacy of expanded projects and responsibilities is necessary to the central authority's process of screening budgetary options. Yet the central authority is asymmetrically ill-informed about the minimum inputs that the bureau needs to achieve any given objective and thus unable to resist the bureau's desire to absorb slack by expanding, even if the central authority lacks confidence in the average and marginal efficiency of the bureau's production process. This conflation of Niskanen with the Carnegie approach is the most coherent explanation we can find of the emergence of white-collar fat in successful (or *once* successful) enterprises whose viability does not demand cost-minimization.

Notice how Niskanen's bureaucratic expansionism interacts with the difficulty of measuring white-collar productivity. A popular commonplace holds that bureaus tend to create work for each other, as each pushes its own agenda at the expense of the agendas of other bureaus. Bureau *A* expands its tasks by devising new types of information to gather and analyze, causing Bureau *B* to expand its staff in order to provide the information. Bureaus' rates of memo production become strategic complements, and high rates of nominal productivity can correspond to substantive stalemate and inaction for the enterprise.

The hypothesis that organizational fat accumulates in successful business enterprises will surprise no reader of journalistic accounts of the troubles of General Motors, IBM, and the like.[19] A theme that surfaces in the literature on U.S. competitiveness is that American enterprises succumb to foreign competitors because of Niskanen-type bureaucratic insularity and noncooperation within enterprises.[20] Most of the academic evidence that supports the hypothesis comes from investigations of the market for corporate control and will be noted subsequently. Working with British data, Nickell, Wadhwani, and Wall found that high debt-equity ratios favor both levels and growth rates of productivity.[21] Caves and Barton found that the inefficiency (gap between average and best-practice productivity) of U.S. manufacturing industries in 1977 increased significantly with the extent of "inbound diversification"—control of establishments by enterprises based in other industries—although it was unaffected by the absolute sizes of the largest firms based in the industry in question.[22]

2.4. RESEARCH DESIGN: NONPRODUCTION EMPLOYMENT AND COMPETITIVE DISTURBANCES

We first analyze the determinants of changes in nonproduction employment in U.S. manufacturing industries during 1972-1986. Specifically we inquire whether white-collar employment was affected by rent-threatening disturbances—international competition and activity in the market for corporate control—after we control for the principal determinants of changes in equilibrium nonproduction employment. This effect of corporate-control changes on the firm's nonproduction employment has already been studied. It is important, however, to pursue the analysis to the level of the industry:

1. The significant downsizing that follows changes in control of the firm might or might not exert a substantial effect at the level of its industry. Downsizings inflicted on particular firms might represent merely part of the constant churning of an industry's size distribution of firms, whereby some leaders lose their grip and regress to the mean, to be replaced by today's comers. Are industries affected as a whole?

2. The disciplinary effect of corporate-control changes is often thought to spill over to onlookers. Whether witnesses are chastened by demonstrations observed in their industries, their cities, or their country clubs is unknown. As a first cut, it seems worth testing whether an industry's nonproduction employment decreases with the assets of that industry's firms subject to current and recent changes in control.

3. An industry as a whole sometimes faces a major disturbance that shrinks its member firms' expected cash flows. The major step-ups in import competition that have afflicted numerous oligopolies in U.S. manufacturing are a conspicuous example. When such a disturbance could excise fat from all of an industry's firms (in addition to the employment change directly associated with the induced change in the industry's output), it becomes desirable to test the hypothesis at the industry level and to ignore any incidental reallocation of activity among its member firms.

4. Data on nonproduction employment are not available at the level of the firm, but data that include administrative and auxiliary establishments can be constructed for manufacturing industries from published Census data.

5. We estimated a model of the determinants of changes in nonproduction workers in U.S. three-digit manufacturing industries over the period 1967-1986, testing whether they are affected by disturbances that could make excess nonproduction employment less viable. It did not prove feasible to develop a structural model to capture shifts in nonproduction-labor demand and supply that should affect these changes. We do control for the putative determinants of demand changes—changes in real output and relative input prices—in testing whether an industry's white-collar employment declined following in-

creases in its import competition and/or in its rate of turnover in corporate control. Was the shrinkage greater in sectors that were *a priori* more likely to run to fat? We set forth the details of the research design in the course of explaining its various features.

Quinquennial Changes 1967-1986

The panel structure utilizes proportional changes over the periods of the successive Censuses of Manufactures, 1967 to 1972, 1972 to 1977, 1977 to 1982, and 1982 to 1986. That is, the dependent variable to be explained will be the logarithm of the number of nonproduction employees in the terminal year minus the logarithm of the number in the initial year. Five-year intervals were judgmentally selected for investigation. We were not interested in the short-run issues associated with labor hoarding and partial adjustment processes, and we believed that important but slow-acting disturbances to nonproduction employment that could be detected from differences among these four quinquennial changes. The 1967-1986 span of the analysis was driven by data considerations. The years 1972 to 1986 provide the core of our data set. The Standard Industrial Classification underwent a moderate change in 1972, limiting the number of three-digit industries that could be traced back to 1967, but we nonetheless made use of 1967-1972 as a base period with broadly normal economic conditions; it was not subject to the inflation of the 1970s, and the main force of increased import competition and disciplinary transactions in the market for corporate control was still to come. With regret we closed the analysis in 1986 because of a major overhaul of the Standard Industrial Classification for the 1987 Census of Manufactures and the termination of our data source on import competition. The descriptive evidence cited previously suggests that the 1980s' squeeze on white-collar employment was strongly felt before 1986, but the process has apparently continued to this day. Indeed, the data for 1986 are cobbled together from 1986 observations on some variables, but for others 1987 observations converted to a 1986 basis on the assumption that constant rates of change were constant between 1982 and 1987.

Production and Administrative Establishments and Industry Classification

We wanted to analyze industries disaggregated into well-defined product markets, which usually means four-digit industries in the Standard Industrial Classification. However, for this analysis it is vital to include not only the nonproduction employees attached to manufacturing establishments (reported at the four-digit level) but also nonproduction employees in auxiliary establishments (allocated by the Census Bureau to three-digit but not four-digit industries). Not only are many nonproduction employees of large companies located away from plants in central administrative establishments and other office facilities, but also the proportion of white-collar employees working at nonfactory locations has risen steadily over the years.[23] When four-digit data are aggregated to the three-digit level only a modest loss of information occurs. Auxiliary-establishment employees, however, toil for firms whose activities might be spread over many four-digit industries, and this diversification necessarily injects substantial noise. Another relevant (and regretted) factor is the less-than-credible jumps observed in some industries' auxiliary-establishment data from census to census. The reclassification of a few large firms between industries could cause jumps, of course, but doubts begin to gnaw when the jumps occur in data on industries little involved in diversification, or when (for example) similar values for 1972 and 1982 surround a divergent value reported for 1977. For these reasons we estimated each model twice, once with the dependent variable based on total nonproduction employees and once on only those based at manufacturing establishments (for which the data seem free of this problem). A statistical relationship significant for the latter could be insignificant for the former due to noisy data rather than a false hypothesis.[24]

Controlling for Demand and Supply Shifts

We should control for other demand and supply factors affecting changes in industries' equilibrium nonproduction employment. Supply factors operating systematically at the industry level are not readily identified, but the determinants of the demand for labor are well worked out in the literature. Hamermesh pointed out that with the assumption of a constant-elasticity-of-substitution production function the demand for labor in the multifactor case can be written:

$$(1)\ \ln L = a_0 + \Sigma b_i(\ln w_i) + a_1(\ln Y) + u$$

where L represents the number of nonproduction employees, w_i the wages of nonproduction workers and any other inputs deemed substitutable for or complementary to them, and Y real output. We borrow this specification with the variables expressed (as explained previously) as proportional changes over Census intervals, but including the key disturbances as additive variables.[25]

We took the simple approach of assuming that white-collar workers are substitutable for production workers but neither a substitute for nor a complement of physical capital and purchased inputs. Substitution between production and nonproduction employees has been confirmed statistically.[26] Evidence available when this project was formulated (summarized by Hamermesh) suggested no confirmed empirical relation between nonproduction employment and capital. Unfortunately, recent evidence from Berndt, Morrison, and Rosenblum and Berman, Bound, and Griliches indicates a significant complementarity between capital and skill, and Brynjolfsson and Hitt concluded that computer capital and related labor have recently been more productive than other inputs (presumably substituting for them).[27] The cost of capital accordingly is an omitted variable in our analysis, though we take slight comfort in the judgment of Berman, Bound, and Griliches that capital-skill complementarity is a small effect. To control for changes in relative factor prices we include only the difference between the proportional changes in salaries per nonproduction worker and wages per production worker over each five-year period.[28]

Sources of Disturbances: Changes in Corporate Control

To test the effect of major shifts in competitive conditions on nonproduction employment we focused on two factors, the changing volume of activity in the market for corporate control and the changes (largely increases) in imports' share of U.S. supplies of manufactured products. The evidence on how changes in corporate control affect efficiency has been accumulating rapidly. Ravenscraft and Scherer showed that those businesses of the four hundred largest enterprises which had undergone control changes before 1973-1977—presumably in the wave of conglomerate mergers in the 1960s—were suffering subnormal performance that deteriorated up to the time of their divestment.[29] Overall, however, changes in control have been found to increase productivity at the establishment level in both the United States and Canada, and Lichtenberg and Siegel estimated that during 1977-1982 the growth of employment in auxiliary establishments of manufacturing enterprises subject to changes in control was 15.7 percent less than in such establishments not undergoing changes in control.[30] For large mergers in the 1980s the subsequent improvement in (industry-normalized) profitability has been associated with better utilization of assets and with reduced employment, especially of white-collar labor.[31]

Arguably these results are all consistent: conglomerate mergers in the 1960s depressed efficiency and productivity while control changes in the late 1970s and 1980s performed a salutary disciplinary function. We organized our test to permit the detection of this pattern. We built up (laboriously) a set of data on the proportions of assets classified to each industry that were subject to changes in control in each year from 1965 to 1986, distinguishing between acquisitions that consolidated related and unrelated activities. For 1979 and before we used the Federal Trade Commission's well-known series, treating their "conglomerate" category as unrelated and all others as related. For years since the FTC data terminated (1980-1986) we sought to replicate the FTC's data-assembly procedure, relying mainly on the ADP data base to identify control changes and the target's base industry. These data suffer to many shortcomings: mergers for which the value of the acquired assets is unknown are missed, and both the FTC and subsequent data are surely incomplete in other ways as well. Because of the massive investment that would be needed to effect major improvements, however, we can only place our faith in the randomness of the errors and omissions.[32]

Thus, the hypothesis that we test is that an industry's usage of non-production labor was shifted by the incidence (proportion of assets involved) of related and unrelated mergers. A two-year lag was judgmentally introduced: the 1967-1972 change in nonproduction employment is related to the summed proportion of industry assets affected during 1966-1970. Whether the proportional volume of activity in the corporate-control market is better related to the change or the level of its nonproduction employment is open to debate, but a prominent consideration is that most of the variance in corporate-control activity is interindustry rather than intertemporal. Notice the important difference between the hypothesis formulated in our study and the predecessors. We observe the assets subject to control changes not in isolation but only as a component of their three-digit industry. The strength of any effects that we observe therefore will depend not just on effects on the business assets directly involved (documented in previous studies) but also effects on competing firms. If after disciplinary control changes the excess employees were dispersed to the more efficient competitors of the taken-over firms, we would observe no effect on industry employment. If instead the takeover of competitors causes sinning rivals to repent and effect their own reforms before the raider strikes, we would find effects that go beyond those measured by Lichtenberg and Siegel.

Sources of Disturbance: Import Competition

The other source of disturbance expected to shift an industry's use of nonproduction labor is import competition. The effect in question here is not the competing down of domestic producers, which is already controlled through inclusion of the industry's real output. Rather, we seek to determine whether changes in international competition alter the effective pressure on producers to minimize the costs of whatever output they offer.

Previous evidence suggests that toughened international competition increases the pressure for cost minimization. International competition reduces the rents obtained by producers in concentrated industries, after control for the degree to which oligopolies' elevated prices themselves attract the import competition.[33] The compressed rents could be an incentive to increase efficiency in the use of nonproduction workers (and other ways), although the relationship between import competition and concentrated industries' rents tells nothing directly about the effect of import competition on efficiency (indeed, it is consistent with consequent reductions in efficiency). Evidence for Canada showed that tariff protection increases the prices set by concentrated Canadian producers relative to their U.S. competitors but not their profit margins, suggesting that protection nurtures inefficiency.[34] Studies of productive efficiency (the gap between average and best-practice productivity in an industry's plants) in six countries found in every case either a positive association of efficiency with import competition or a negative association with restrictions on import competition.[35]

Because the efficient use of nonproduction workers seems particularly problematical for large firms, an apt question is whether import competition tends to take a greater toll of the large or small competitors in any given industry. This can be inferred from the way in which seller concentration changes with import competition once the change in domestic industry output is controlled. On average the smaller producers take the worse hit (that is, concentration increases). However, that pattern is mitigated or reversed in industries that are intensive in skilled labor, physical capital, and sales-promotion activities. The induced reductions in concentration in these industries appear to be due to changes in the relative sizes of large and small companies more than to changes in the numbers of companies or establishments. Industries with these activity structures are probably the most susceptible to the inefficient use of nonproduction labor.[36]

The pressure for cost-cutting brought by import competition might be evident in patterns of employee compensation, where wages might be constricted through the effects of import competition on employees' rents or quasi-rents. During the 1980s wages became responsive to industry-level demand shifts associated with international competition. The effects can be explained by shifts in sectors' real outputs, however, and we are aware of no evidence that distinguishes between output changes and intensified incentives to minimize the cost of producing any given output.[37]

To obtain data on imports matched to production is problematical for the United States, because the trade statistics (recorded on a commodity-based classification) are not readily matched to the production statistics (establishment basis). The match on which we relied, prepared by the U.S. International Trade Administration, is available for the years 1972-1986.

To recapitulate, the basic regression model takes the form:

$$\text{NPRA} = a_0 + a_1\text{QR} + a_2\text{WDIFR} + a_3\text{IMPR} + a_4\text{MERGR} + a_5\text{MERGU} + u$$

where

NPRA=   logarithm of final-year nonproduction-worker employment minus logarithm of initial-year nonproduction worker employment, including employment in auxiliary establishments;

QR=   logarithm of final-year real output minus logarithm of initial-year real output;

WDIFR=   (logarithm of final-year salary per nonproduction worker minus logarithm of initial-year salary per nonproduction worker) minus (logarithm of final-year average annual wage per production worker minus logarithm of initial-year average annual wage per production worker);

IMPR=   ratio of value of competing imports to total supply (imports plus production) in terminal year minus ratio of value of imports to total supply in initial year);

MERGR=   proportion of industry assets absorbed in related
                    mergers between initial and terminal years, lagged
                    two years;

MERGU=   proportion of industry assets absorbed in unrelated
                    mergers between initial and terminal years, lagged
                    two years.

A dummy variable is included for each time period (D77 designates
1972-1977 observations, etc.). Their inclusion is particularly important
because the census years fall at diverse points in the business cycle.
Dummy variables (not reported in the tables) are also included for 18
of the 20 two-digit manufacturing industries (each of the two omitted
industries, tobacco and petroleum, is represented by a single three-digit
industry); with at most four observations in the time dimension, a fixed
effect for each three-digit industry was likely to leave little variance for
the substantive regressors.

    NPRA and QR can clearly be affected by common disturbances,
and the substantive framework of this investigation hardly rejects the
possibility that WDIFR might be causally affected by NPRA. Initially
we hoped to use instrumental variables to avoid the biased and inconsistent estimates that ordinary least squares would yield in such circumstances. Experiments at instrumenting QR did not work well, however, and no approach to instrumenting WDIFR seemed attractive even
ex ante.[38] Our concern is not with estimating a demand function for
nonproduction labor, however, but only with determining whether
major shocks changed its usage. Ordinary least squares recovers the
best predictor of the effects of these shocks on the conditional mean of
the dependent variable, and so should suffice for our main purpose.

    Deficiencies of the data cause us to report several versions of each
model. First, although the change in nonproduction employment is in
principle better measured with administrative establishments included,
the diversification of large enterprises and disturbing discontinuities in
the data (mentioned previously) make it possible that noise in these
establishments' data could obscure significant relationships. Therefore
we also estimated each model on the change in nonproduction employ-

ees working in production establishments (the dependent variable is then designated NPR rather than NPRA). (The relative-compensation variable WDIFR is measured as a weighted average of production and administrative establishments' average-compensation data in the former case, only from manufacturing establishments in the latter.)[39] Second, observations on IMPR (change in import competition) are unavailable before 1972, so we estimate each model with and without IMPR (and the dummy for the 1972-1977 period) included.

2.5. STATISTICAL RESULTS: DETERMINANTS OF CHANGES IN NONPRODUCTION EMPLOYMENT

To preview the flavor of our conclusions, the effects of the corporate-control market and of import competition differ among types of industries and periods of time. After the core results in Table 2.4 are noted, we turn to the pursuit of slope shifts that expose these differential effects. Heteroskedasticity-consistent standard errors are used to calculate the reported t-statistics.

To take the control variables first, the growth of nonproduction employment is closely associated with the growth rates of industries' real outputs. Employees in auxiliary establishments are more likely to perform truly overhead functions than nonproduction workers based at manufacturing locations and, accordingly, the estimated elasticities with respect to output are higher by 15 to 20 percent when the former are excluded. The coefficient of the change in the nonproduction-to-production worker wage ratio is correctly negative. It is significant when central-office employees are omitted but not when they are included. Several reasons for the divergent significance levels suggest themselves: (1) opportunities for substituting between nonproduction and production workers might be concentrated in establishments where both are employed; (2) industry-level wage differentials are probably measured with less error in manufacturing plants than in central office establishments; (3) nonproduction employment in central offices might be less sensitive to labor-cost variations, or employee compensation might contain a larger endogenous component. A positive intercept

Table 2.4

Determinants of changes in nonproduction employment: basic model

Exogenous variable	Endogenous variable			
	NRPA	NRP	NRPA	NRP
Constant	0.141	0.075	0.199	0.118
	(1.31)	(1.51)	(1.49)	(2.11)
QR	0.456	0.543	0.382	0.481
	(8.81)	(14.08)	(7.01)	(11.06)
WDIFR	-0.149	-0.373	-0.186	-0.425
	(0.83)	(3.28)	(0.93)	(3.31)
MERGR	-0.0007	-0.0007	-0.0012	-0.0007
	(0.82)	(0.93)	(1.15)	(0.70)
MERGU	0.0002	0.0006	0.0017	0.0008
	(0.38)	(1.71)	(1.44)	(1.09)
IMPR	—	—	-0.0010	-0.0004
			(0.84)	(0.53)
D77	0.019	0.027	—	—
	(0.82)	(1.66)		
D82	0.076	0.067	0.046	0.029
	(3.11)	(3.83)	(2.10)	(1.78)
D86	-0.128	-0.075	-0.134	-0.097
	(3.51)	(3.85)	(3.84)	(4.74)
	+ 18 dummies	+ 18 dummies	+ 18 dummies	+ 18 dummies
R^2	0.320	0.551	0.292	0.524
No. obs.	351	434	282	342

Note: t-statistics appear in parentheses.

shift is observed for the 1977-1982 period, a negative one for 1982-1986. The pattern conforms to the impression that a recent squeeze-out following an earlier build-up, but of course the recession-year status of 1982 is a sufficient explanation.

In Table 2.4 the measures of activity in the market for corporate control are not particularly significant. Related mergers apparently reduce nonproduction employment and unrelated ones increase it, but at most the coefficients achieve 10-percent significance in a two-tail test. Similarly the sign of the effect of changes in import competition is cor-

rect, but it is not significant. Our principal hypotheses about disciplinary forces thus are not accepted for all sectors and time periods, but
they might prevail in *a priori* congenial times and industrial settings.

Variations over Time

That the key hypotheses fail to win support for the whole time period is
not a big surprise. Import competition struck U.S. industries at diverse
times but clearly stepped up over the period of analysis. Mergers, unrelated ones in particular, surely varied in their consequences between
the go-go conglomerates of the late 1960s and the bust-up takeovers of
the 1980s. The findings of Blair and Schary support the impression that
efficiency-increasing reorganizations accelerated greatly in the
1980s—a phenomenon that they tied to the encroachment of high real
interest rates on free cash flows.[40]

Table 2.5 on the following page, reports models that allow for
slope shifts over time in the model's various coefficients; this treatment
is applied to one variable at a time, to avoid clutter. Each regressor was
multiplied by dummy variables set equal to one for 1972-1977, 1977-
1982, and 1982-1986 in turn (only the latter two periods for IMPR).
Each independent variable's slope shifts are reported in a separate pair
of equations in Table 2.5. For QR the slope shifts in equations (1) and
(2) are negative and generally significant, although 1982-1986 shows
no significant shift. These results need to be considered in relation to
the intercept shifts. Together they indicate that during 1972-1982 nonproduction employment grew but in ways not related to changes in
industries' real outputs. One possibility to be investigated below is that
differential behavior of industries with rising and falling outputs could
explain this pattern. For the change in relative compensation levels
(WDIFR) the significant negative effect found in Table 2.4 is evident
in manufacturing establishments from 1972 on but not previously. We
conjecture that the pattern results from the greater variance of WDIFR
observed in the inflationary conditions of 1972-1982, and the data
partly support the conjecture.[41]

Table 2.5
Stability over time of coefficients of determinants of changes in nonproduction employment

Exogenous variable	Endogenous variable							
	NPRA (1)	NPR (2)	NPRA (3)	NPR (4)	NPRA (5)	NPR (6)	NPRA (7)	NPR (8)
Constant	0.124 (1.14)	0.066 (1.27)	0.153 (1.42)	0.088 (1.67)	0.136 (1.30)	0.074 (1.46)	0.182 (1.37)	0.112 (1.98)
QR	0.592 (7.23)	0.652 (13.34)	0.460 (8.75)	0.551 (14.16)	0.456 (8.92)	0.546 (14.12)	0.403 (7.87)	0.484 (11.44)
WDIFR	-0.134 (0.76)	-0.335 (2.98)	0.110 (0.28)	0.174 (0.78)	-0.214 (1.44)	-0.378 (3.35)	-0.177 (0.90)	-0.404 (3.20)
MERGR	-0.0008 (0.91)	-0.0008 (1.05)	-0.0006 (0.67)	-0.0006 (0.77)	-0.0006 (0.69)	-0.0008 (0.98)	-0.0011 (1.15)	-0.0006 (0.66)
MERGU	0.0003 (0.51)	0.0006 (1.37)	0.0004 (0.61)	0.0008 (2.12)	-0.0005 (0.71)	0.0007 (1.77)	0.002 (1.76)	0.0009 (1.15)
D77	0.043 (1.66)	0.049 (2.64)	0.008 (0.30)	0.008 (0.43)	0.013 (0.51)	0.025 (1.51)	—	—
D82	0.090 (3.95)	0.075 (4.51)	0.066 (2.73)	0.042 (2.05)	0.065 (2.51)	0.063 (3.44)	0.043 (2.05)	0.025 (1.59)
D86	-0.114 (3.17)	-0.075 (3.65)	-0.145 (4.23)	-0.099 (5.06)	-0.106 (3.00)	-0.072 (3.62)	-0.087 (2.47)	-0.081 (3.97)
QRD77	-0.188 (1.23)	-0.208 (2.14)						
QRD82	-0.208 (2.18)	-0.233 (3.46)						
QRD86	-0.078 (0.33)	-0.057 (0.59)						

Table 2.5 (continued)
Stability over time of coefficients of determinants of changes in nonproduction employment

Exogenous variable	Endogenous variable							
	NPRA (1)	NPR (2)	NPRA (3)	NPR (4)	NPRA (5)	NPR (6)	NPRA (7)	NPR (8)
WDIFD77			-0.653 (1.39)	-0.775 (2.50)				
WDIFD82			-0.326 (0.77)	-0.717 (2.74)				
WDIFD86			0.049 (0.11)	-0.377 (1.40)				
MGUD77					0.002 (1.76)	0.0006 (0.53)		
MGUD82					0.003 (1.40)	0.002 (1.54)		
MGUD86					-0.023 (2.48)	-0.0001 (2.05)		
IMPR					-0.0007 (1.62)	0.0006 (0.73)		
IMPD82							0.0023 (1.59)	0.0020 (1.62)
IMPD86							-0.007 (5.24)	-0.024 (1.91)
	+18 dummies	+18 dummies	+18 dummies	+18 dummies	+18 dummies	+18 dummies	+18 dummies	+18 dummies
R^2	0.322	0.568	0.330	0.562	0.328	0.550	0.326	0.548
No.obs.	351	434	351	434	351	434	282	342

Note: t-statistics appear in parentheses.

When slope shifts are added for related mergers none is significant, but the negative effect in manufacturing establishments overall
(i.e. the base coefficient of MERGR) becomes significant at 10 percent
(not shown in Table 2.5). Related mergers would seem generally to
economize on white-collar employees,[42] but they did not propel the
squeeze-out during the 1980s. The finding accords with the view that
such mergers chiefly involve the redeployment of firms' lumpy and
intangible assets rather than serving a disciplinary role in corporate
governance. For unrelated mergers the results are more dramatic.
Equations (5) and (6) both suggest that unrelated mergers were associated with increasing white-collar employment during 1972-1982 (weak
statistical significance) but with decreasing white-collar employment
during the 1980s (significant).

This pattern is consistent with unsuccessful, fat-promoting diversified mergers in the 1960s and 1970s giving way to bust-up (fat-
shedding) takeovers in the 1980s.[43] The commonplace interpretation of
a bust-up role for unrelated acquisitions in the 1980s is thus confirmed.
Although these results are not surprising when regarded as effects of
control changes on target firms, it is significant that they prevail at the
three-digit industry level. They are not washed out in the churning of
firm sizes (employment) within an industry, and/or they are amplified
by contagion. The effects of both related and unrelated mergers, although subject to great uncertainty, appear to be quantitatively substantial.

The effect of IMPR appears initially to be positive (weakly significant) during 1977-1982 but grows significantly negative after 1982.
During 1982-1986 an increase of five percentage points in an industry's
ratio of imports to total supply apparently caused a 1 to 4 percent decline in nonproduction employment (the higher figure estimated when
administrative establishments are included). The effect cannot be due
to the substitution of production for nonproduction labor, because
Berman, Bound, and Griliches showed that increases in imports' market
share were associated with the upgrading of an industry's skill mix
(their analysis covered 1979-1987). The result is consistent with Mac-
Donald's conclusions about the effects of import competition on productivity.[44] Finally, the result can be contrasted to the findings of

Scherer and Huh about R&D activities of U.S. manufacturers in the face of international competition—initially a submissive reaction followed by a provoked one.[45]

Variations among Sectors and Settings

If disciplining effects can be localized in time, can they also be localized by sectors with certain market structures? If surplus staff accumulates solely due to the preferences of poorly monitored managers, it should be randomly distributed among market structures (once we control for the prevalence of the corporate form of organization). The Carnegie-Niskanen approach, however, suggests that some market structures might be more congenial to business corpulence—where white-collar tasks are important in firms' activities, and where these tasks require the collaboration of diverse nonproduction specialists and skills.

We related a group of market-structure traits that might distinguish sectoral environments having these traits (a single observation on each industry centered in our time period):

R   Total research and development outlays of the industry divided by value of shipments and outward transfers, 1977;

A   Total media advertising outlays and other sales-promotion outlays divided by value of shipments and outward transfers, 1977;

K   For each quinquennial census period, the sum of nominal capital expenditures at establishments classified to the industry divided by the sum of (nominal) values of industry shipments in the same years;

C   Four-firm producer concentration ratio for the industry in 1977 (industry-shipments-weighted average of ratios for four-digit industries classified to each three-digit industry);

S   Combined size (value of shipments) of the four leading firms
     in each four-digit industry, converted to a weighted average
     for the three-digit industry using industry shipments as weight.

Employing the simplest possible approach, we calculated the median
value for each of these variables, formed a dummy variable (D_i) set
equal to one if the industry ranks above the sample median, zero otherwise. The product of D_i and one of the regressors embodying disturbances then serves to test the hypothesis that the disturbance's effect
differs significantly between the industries ranked low and high on the
*i*th structural attribute (the dummy is also entered to allow an intercept
shift).

Table 2.6 on the following pages, reports re-estimations of the
basic model (Table 2.4) to test these structural shifts, with the reported
equations truncated to the coefficients directly involved (other coefficients were not substantially changed from Table 2.4). Equations 1 and
2 show that related mergers in industries with low research-intensities
are associated with decreased use of white-collar labor, while in industries with above-median R&D levels the effect shifts to positive. Similar patterns appear for advertising (equations 3, 4) and for investment-
intensity as it affects central-office employees (equation 5) but not
those in manufacturing plant (equation 6). We expect R, A, and K all to
be positively correlated with producer concentration, and indeed equations 7 and 8 show that related mergers are also associated with higher
white-collar employment in the more concentrated industries. The average size of an industry's leading firms has a similar effect with related
mergers tending to increase white-collar employment in industries with
large leading firms (weak statistical significance in equations 9 and 10).
In contrast to these findings on related mergers, industry-structure differences do not alter the effects of unrelated mergers in any significant
or even regular way. The only exception (equations 11 and 12) is that
unrelated mergers have tended to sustain increased white-collar employment when they take place in concentrated industries (weakly significant).

Do the results on mergers and mediating structural conditions tell a
coherent story? The difference between the patterns for related and

Table 2.6
Dependence of effect of shifters of nonproduction-labor demand on characteristics of industry structure

Dependent variable	Interactive exogenous variables			R^2	Number of observations
1. NPRA	-0.0019 MERGR + (1.95)	0.0046 DRMERGR - (2.58)	0.039 DR (1.53)	0.320	348
2. NPR	-0.0028 MERGR + (3.19)	0.0040 DRMERGR - (3.66)	0.039 DR (2.40)	0.563	431
3. NPRA	-0.0014 MERGR + (1.60)	0.0023 DAMERGR - (1.38)	0.027 DA (1.02)	0.313	348
4. NPR	-0.0012 MERGR + (1.27)	0.0013 DAMERGR - (0.83)	0.013 DA (0.78)	0.547	431
5. NPRA	-0.0017 MERGR + (1.10)	0.0010 DKMERGR + (0.54)	0.034 DK (1.67)	0.321	351
6. NPR	0.0006 MERGR - (0.66)	0.0026 DKMERGR + (2.21)	0.025 DK (0.23)	0.557	434
7. NPRA	-0.0025 MERGR + (2.66)	0.0043 DCMERGR - (3.26)	0.030 DC (3.53)	0.327	351
8. NRP	-0.0016 MERGR + (1.65)	0.0027 DCMERGR - (2.02)	0.019 DC (1.26)	0.556	434
9. NPRA	-0.0016 MERGR + (1.85)	0.0025 DSMERGR - (1.54)	0.043 DS (0.22)	0.323	351
10. NPR	-0.0016 MERGR + (1.66)	0.0021 DSMERGR - (1.77)	0.045 DS (2.88)	0.560	434
11. NPRA	-0.0002 MERGU + (0.27)	0.0028 DCMERGU - (1.73)	0.019 DC (0.82)	0.318	351

Table 2.6
(*continued*)
Dependence of effect of shifters of nonproduction-labor demand on characteristics of industry structure

Dependent variable	Interactive exogenous variables			R^2	Number of observations
12. NPR	-0.0004 MERGU + (0.97)	0.0028 DCMERGU - (1.43)	0.011 DC (0.75)	0.551	434
13. NPRA	0.0012 IMPR - (1.00)	0.0037 DCIMPR - (1.40)	0.008 DC (0.30)	0.293	282
14. NPR	-0.0013 IMPR + (1.53)	0.0018 DCIMPR - (1.44)	0.010 DC (0.60)	0.528	342
15. NPRA	0.0002 IMPR - (0.13)	0.0038 DSIMPR - (1.61)	0.026 DS (0.96)	0.302	282
16. NPR	-0.0002 IMPR - (0.23)	0.0013 DSIMPR - (0.59)	0.026 DS (1.49)	0.527	342

unrelated mergers tells us that the effects of mergers on white-collar employment are associated with the redeployment of assets and activities that we expect to be associated with related mergers. Related mergers economize on nonproduction labor inputs in activities where that input is less important in the first place, but they can augment it where it is important. Thus, the normative implications of related mergers' positive effects on white-collar employment are ambiguous: it seems desirable in research-intensive industries but not in concentrated industries. Conversely, whatever the typical effects of unrelated mergers, they are independent of the industry structures and activity patterns that in turn govern the payout from asset redeployments associated with mergers (as Table 2.5 showed, however, unrelated mergers' effects have varied substantially over time). That unrelated mergers have not compressed white-collar employment in concentrated industries (equation 11) seems anomalous, but other (negative) results on slope shifts for MERGU (and equations 5 and 6 of Table 2.5) incline us to put this result aside.

The mediating effect of structural conditions on the slope coefficient form IMPR can be considered more briefly. As equations 13-16 of Table 2.6 show, import competition seems to squeeze employment in central office establishments, as indicated by negative effects on NPRA in large-firm industries that are not observed when the dependent variable reflects only plant-based nonproduction employment (NPR). The result is consistent with Niskanen's bureaucracy hypothesis and with the doleful tales of corporate downsizing heard in the 1980s.

The evidence of Table 2.6 suggests that a firm's susceptibility to inflated white-collar employment might depend on the activities mandated by its industry's structure. The linkages are quite explicable in the case of mergers. But they are not strong statistically, and leave room for the hypothesis that corporate governance chiefly matters for efficiency, not the firm's structure of activities. In the next section we get another shot at testing for structural differences in proneness to corporate obesity.

2.6. DOWNSIZING EMPLOYMENT:
A FIRM-LEVEL ANALYSIS

Overall, this inquiry has provided some support for the hypothesis that some U.S. corporations accumulated excess nonproduction employees that they were forced to disgorge by exogenously increased pressures to minimize costs. The statistical effects occurred at times and (to a modest extent) in sectors where they might have been expected. We are thus inclined to reject the null hypothesis about accumulated organizational slack, although data limitations qualify the results, and value-maximizing explanations for these statistical patterns cannot be ruled out.

This retrospective analysis suggests that at least some corporate downsizing should raise expected profits. We now address that question directly by measuring and analyzing stock-market reactions to the announcements of corporate downsizings. Have positive reactions been common? Have they occurred in settings where the downsizing might likely remove corporate fat rather than acknowledge corporate misfortune?

Possible Reactions to Announcements of Downsizing

How the market reacts to downsizing announcements might be explained in these two ways:

1. *Asymmetrical information.* If managers are value maximizers and they and shareholders are equally well-informed, downsizings will occur at optimal times and shareholders should have no systematic reactions to their announcements (as distinguished from the adverse shocks that induced the downsizings). Keep the assumption that managers are value maximizers able to choose and sustain intendedly optimal levels of nonproduction employment. Suppose, however, that managers have better information than the general public about the firm's future profit prospects, and that states of nature in which the firm's (flow) profits will be reduced are highly correlated with circumstances in which its optimal employment level is lowered.[46] The downsizing announcement then serves to reveal to the market bad news

that management has already received and is acting upon. The market's reaction to the downsizing announcement should be negative if this "bad news" effect dominates.

2. *Excision of slack.* Assume that white-collar employment and cooperating resources can be inflated in a successful firm in the manner described previously. Assume that the excess cost's existence is known to owners of the firm's equity and capitalized (negatively) into the value of the shares. A downsizing announcement then can raise the value of the firm's shares by revealing that some coalition-breaking force has dislodged the unproductive resources. This "bite the bullet" effect could arise from disgorging resources other than white-collar employees, such as unprofitable activities retained for the utility they give to managers.[47]

These opposed sign predictions leave us with no prior about the mean value of the excess returns associated with announcements of corporate downsizings.[48] The preceding part of this paper indicated that some firms are forced to bite the bullet, but these cases need not account for many or even a large proportion of downsizings. Furthermore, a downsizing judged by shareholders to have bite-the-bullet significance could at the same time reveal bad news and adduce a negative market reaction. Therefore the mean value of excess returns associated with downsizing announcements is unlikely to discriminate between the hypotheses. All owners can be assumed to share a common reaction to a given announcement, so we expect the variance of the excess returns to reflect the differing situations of the announcing firms. In the balance of this section we report the first phase of this investigation.

Research Design and Core Results

We collected a sample of announcements of corporate downsizings appearing in the *Wall Street Journal* between 1987 and 1991 by searching the ABI/Inform data base for stories reporting layoffs and retaining all announcements that mentioned specific quantitative layoff targets. This process yielded a total of 513 announcements of downsizings by U.S. corporations whose excess returns are available on the data tape of the Center for Research in Securities Prices. These excess returns were obtained for the day of the announcement (XR0) and for three trading days before (XRM1–XRM3) and three trading days subsequently (XRP1–XRP3). Their means and standard errors are shown in Table 2.7. The average downsizing announcement brings a loss of 0.63 percent of the company's value on the announcement date, anticipated by losses on the two previous trading days that bring the total to 1.65 percent. The mean return on each of these three days differs significantly from zero at the 5 percent level. The concentration of significant excess returns on the announcement date and the two preceding days agrees with the pattern found by Blackwell, Marr, and Spivey, and the sum of excess returns over this three-day "window" will be the dependent variable that we seek to explain subsequently.[49] About 60 percent of the three-day returns are negative (mean = -5.1 percent) while 40 percent are positive (mean = 3.7 percent). The enlarged standard errors at the time of announcement are consistent with the perspective offered above: the different situations of individual companies could cause downsizing announcements to adduce widely varying market reactions.

We recorded whether several attributes were present in or missing from the announcements of downsizings. The attributes were picked to shed light on the prevalence of bad-news and bite-the-bullet effects. The proportions of announcements including each attributed are reported in Table 2.7, along with means of the three-day returns for observations with and without them. Consider first the features that indicate the magnitude of the adverse shock and should be associated with lower (more negative) excess returns. The announcement indicated that a charge would be taken against earnings to cover the costs of the downsizing in 19 percent of the cases, and these charges resulted in losses of value of 2.96 percent, while firms not announcing charges lost only 1.32 percent. In 14 percent of the news stories earnings were also announced, and negative announced earnings brought a market-value loss of 6.16 percent, while positive earnings slightly mitigated the mean loss of 1.10 percent in cases accompanied by no earnings announcement. Announcement that the employment attrition would be voluntary or temporary brought smaller losses, presumably bringing smaller reductions in the expected present value of the firm's earnings.

Table 2.7
Excess returns associated with corporations' announced decisions to
downsize and properties of announcements

Variable	Proportion of cases	Mean value of excess return	
		With stated property	Without stated property
Excess returns			
XRM3	n.a.	0.061%	(0.39)
	n.a.		
XRM2	n.a.	-0.348	(2.19)
	n.a.		
XRM1	n.a.	-0.681	(3.14)
	n.a.		
XR0	n.a.	-0.625	(2.72)
	n.a.		
XRP1	n.a.	0.430	(1.94)
	n.a.		
XRP2	n.a.	-0.228	(1.41)
	n.a.		
XRP3	n.a.	-0.024	(0.17)
	n.a.		
Features of announcements			
Charge against earnings	19.1%	-2.963	-1.321
Earnings announced	2.7	-0.173	-1.104
Loss announced	11.1	-6.164	
Separations voluntary	20.7	-0.607	-1.900
Separations temporary	11.1	-1.152	-1.692
Previous merger	5.7	-1.123	-1.662
Plant closure	29.0	-1.224	-1.799
Reorganization announced	24.8	-1.414	-1.703
White-collar layoffs	30.2	-0.726	-2.026

Note: t-statistics for mean excess returns appear in parentheses.

We expected that downsizings following mergers would be smaller
losses for having been anticipated, but the mean difference is small.
These differences largely confirm that varying badness of the news
accounts for part of the variance of the excess returns.

The market's responses to other attributes seem to reveal the bite-the-bullet effect. Announcement that the downsizing would involve the closure of a plant should have a depressant effect as new information, but it entailed smaller mean losses (1.22 percent) than when no closure was announced (1.80 percent). The loss is slightly smaller when the layoffs were announced as part of a plan to reorganize, refocus, or consolidate the firm or change its strategy, 1.41 percent rather than 1.70 percent. Most striking, the announcement that white-collar layoffs would be involved produced a smaller loss (0.73 percent) than otherwise (2.03 percent).

We also measured the proportion of the workforce to be laid off. It ranges from 0.01 percent to 53 percent, with a mean of 5.6 percent. This variable is taken from the *Wall Street Journal* story when reported there as a proportion. When it is reported as an absolute number, we converted it to a proportion by using as a divisor the total-employment figure reported for the previous year-end in Standard and Poor's *Compustat PC Plus* data base. The distribution of observations on the proportion laid off (hereafter L) is roughly half-normal, with the mode close to zero. Also, we had reason to expect it to be conditional on the sizes of companies. If (as is commonly assumed) the adjustment costs of reducing a firm's employment are convex in the (absolute) number of employees laid off, we expect the *proportional* sizes of layoffs (L) to have a wider dispersion for small companies than for large. Even without this factor, the *Wall Street Journal* presumably reports small downsizings by large firms and large downsizings by small ones, but not small downsizings by small firms. Because bite-the-bullet effects might be more common among large firms, we were concerned about the interaction between L and firms' employment size (hereafter S). We first regressed three-day excess returns on dummy variables indicating ranges of L, in order to observe the shape of this relation. The regression coefficients and the mean values of S for each tranche of L are:

Proportion laid off L	Regression coefficient (and t-statistic)	Mean S	Number of observations
0 < L < 0.01	omitted class	209,230	177
0.01 < L < 0.02	-0.0097 (1.61)	121,875	69
0.02 < L < 0.03	0.0017 (0.23)	120,506	38
0.03 < L < 0.06	-0.0004 (0.05)	84,806	77
0.06 < L < 0.10	-0.0192 (1.77)	40,129	69
0.10 < L < 0.18	-0.0410 (2.04)	16,638	50
0.18 < L	-0.0530 (2.01)	7,631	33

Announcements of larger layoffs cause more negative reactions, but apparently have no regular effect on market value until they reach a threshold of around 6 percent. A simple linear relation between three-day excess returns and L will turn out to fit the data fairly well, but the preceding regression result shows that it is determined by the larger layoffs announced by the smaller firms in the sample. We investigated whether three-day excess returns are related to S for individual tranches of L but no significant relationships were found.

Determinants of Excess Returns: Regression Analysis

A regression analysis of the determinants of three-day excess returns (XR0 + XRM1 + XRM2) yielded the results shown in Table 2.8.[50] The regressors include those listed in Table 2.7 plus the fraction of employees to be laid off. Equation 2 differs from equation 1 only in excluding the dummy for separations that are temporary, which is never at all significant and is highly collinear with S (because the giant auto firms announce many temporary separations—more on this subsequently). In equation 2 all signs are correct and layoffs (L) and the dummy for reported losses are significant, as are the dummies for voluntary separations and for nonproduction-worker layoffs if one-tail tests are deemed appropriate. The occurrence of a charge against earnings is insignificant because it is strongly collinear with other variables, especially negative earnings. This is quite plausible as the charge represents purely an accounting decision that should be conditional on the resource-allocation decisions registered by the other regressors.

Table 2.8
Regression models of determinants of excess returns associated with corporate downsizing announcements

Exogenous variable	Equation number				
	1	2	3	4	5
Constant	-0.011	-0.012	-0.008	-0.008	-0.005
	(1.97)	(2.23)	(1.64)	(1.94)	(1.05)
Fraction laid off (L)	-0.182	-0.179	-0.225	-0.253	-0.219
	(2.07)	(2.07)	(2.39)	(2.49)	(2.39)
Charge against earnings	-0.004	-0.004	-0.005	-0.005	-0.007
	(0.37)	(0.34)	(0.42)	(0.43)	(0.58)
Loss announced	0.043	-0.043	-0.043	-0.046	-0.040
	(2.17)	(2.17)	(2.17)	(2.32)	(2.05)
Separations voluntary	0.011	0.011	0.010	0.012	0.010
	(1.62)	(1.69)	(1.58)	(1.80)	(1.53)
Separations temporary	-0.005	—	—	—	—
	(0.56)				
Previous merger	-0.004	-0.004	-0.005	-0.004	-0.005
	(0.60)	(0.57)	(0.72)	(0.46)	(0.72)
Plant closure	0.010	0.009	0.007	—	0.007
	(1.27)	(1.28)	(1.01)	(0.97)	

Table 2.8 (*continued*)
Regression models of determinants of excess returns associated with corporate downsizing announcements

Exogenous variable	Equation number				
	1	2	3	4	5
Reorganization announced	0.009 (0.96)	0.010 (1.05)	0.007 (0.77)	0.009 (0.93)	—
White-collar layoffs	0.011 (1.64)	0.012 (1.73)	—	0.011	—
L* White-collar	(2.79)	—	0.289 (1.59)	—	—
l* Plant closure	(2.35)	—	—	0.278	—
L* White-collar*Reorganization	(3.15)	—	—	—	0.384
R^2	0.075	0.077	0.091	0.099	0.092

Note: (t-statistics appear in parentheses; each model is estimated from 512 observations.

Equation 3 interacts the fraction laid off with the dummy indicating white-collar discharges. The interaction's positive coefficient is significant, and its magnitude more than offsets the negative coefficient of the laid-off fraction itself. This finding confirms the hypothesis that the market's positive reactions to downsizing announcements are associated with white-collar separations. In equation 4 the fraction laid off is interacted with the dummy indicating plant closure. The coefficient of the interaction term is again significant and large enough to offset the coefficient of L. This interaction test was performed with the dummy indicating a reorganization was announced, yielding an insignificant coefficient (not shown). In equation 5 the dummy indicating a reorganization announced in shifted from an additive regressor to one multiplied by L and the nonproduction-workers dummy; compared to equation 3, the t-statistic on the interaction and the equation's F-statistic increase.[51] If the sample is subdivided into cases with and without reorganizations announced, the positive coefficient of the dummy indicating white-collar layoffs is significant only when reorganization takes place. The same result occurs when the cases of voluntary and involuntary separations are distinguished: shareholders applaud reduced-white collar employment (significantly) only when actual layoffs are involved.

The results so far support the hypothesis that separations of nonproduction workers are sometimes viewed as creating value for shareholders, but the explanatory power of Table 2.8's models is quite low. Could we increase it by identifying *a priori* a subsample of firms most likely to indulge in excess white-collar employment? In contrast to Table 2.6's approach we selected an indicator based on the firm itself: selling, general, and administrative expenses per employee (SGA) as a measure of the intensity of overhead costs and the potential for Niskanen-type behavior. We ranked the observations for which this variable is available (only 324 of 513), split the sample into firms below and above median SGA, and estimated various models on the subsamples separately.

Table 2.9 on the following page, illustrates the useful conclusions yielded by this exercise. First, the explanatory power of the model is (for such cross-sections) rather good for the high-*SGA* subsample but nonexistent for the downsizings by low-*SGA* firms. By implication, much of the consequence of scale changes for expected profit is bound up in administrative and organizational choices for the former group, other factors for the latter group. The plant-closure dummy is significant for high-*SGA* firms although not in the sample as a whole.

Second, Table 2.9's model for the high-overhead firms allows us to investigate the positive values of the three-day returns in a way that is infeasible with Table 2.8's model. In Table 2.9 the complex relation between excess returns and *L* is successfully represented by a quadratic relationship—a maneuver that does not work (that is, does not improve statistically on a linear representation of *L*) for the whole sample. We can calculate the range of fractions laid off (*L*) for which predicted excess returns are positive, conditional on values of the other regressors, as follows:

1. Set all the dummy variables (including the indicator of white-collar layoffs) equal to zero. Predicted three-day excess returns then are negative for all values of *L*.

2. Set the dummy indicating white-collar layoffs = 1 but all the other dummies equal to zero. Predicted excess returns are then positive for all fractions laid off such that 2.3 percent < *L* < 20.9 percent.

3. Set the dummy indicating the announcement of a reorganization = 1 (in addition to the white-collar dummy), but the others equal to zero. Predicted excess returns are then positive for all values of *L* < 27 percent.[52]

In these overhead-intensive firms it takes the bad news of a very large downsizing to offset the gains that shareholders expect from reducing the white-collar cadre (with or without formal reorganization).

Further Experiments

Several other experiments that were performed with the data base can be summarized briefly:

Table 2.9

Regression models of determinants of excess returns with companies distinguished by importance of overhead activities

Exogenous variable	SGA per employee below median	SGA per employee above median
Constant	-0.011	-0.049
	(1.06)	(3.48)
Fraction laid off (L)	-0.083	0.436
	(0.48)	(1.89)
Charge against earnings	-0.020	-0.027
	(1.46)	(1.32)
Loss announced	0.002	-0.073
	(0.09)	(2.42)
Separations voluntary	0.012	0.018
	(1.15)	(1.80)
Previous merger	0.005	-0.010
	(0.28)	(0.90)
Plant closure	-0.006	0.030
	(0.63)	(1.87)
Reorganization announced	0.001	-0.027
	(0.06)	(1.42)
White-collar layoffs	0.004	0.039
	(0.46)	(2.61)
Layoffs squared (L^2)	0.127	-1.858
	(0.31)	(2.72)
Previous announcements	0.010	0.020
	(1.06)	(1.36)
R^2	-0.006	0.193

Note: t-statistics appear in parentheses; each model is estimated from 162 observations (SGA is available for 324 firms).

1. A chronic problem with studies of this type is that the "event" does not represent a clean injection of completely new information. For example, an announced downsizing might follow upon earlier downsizings that caused shareholders to anticipate that the observed announcement would take place; the excess return then values only the difference between the terms actually announced and those that the market expected (our 512 announcements emanate from only 240 firms). Blackwell, Marr, and Spivey found that significant negative returns were set off by a firm's first plant-closure announcement (in their data base) but not by subsequent announcements (also see Worrell, Davidson, and Sharma). In Table 2.9 we added a dummy indicating layoff announcements successive to the firm's first in our data base (of course, not necessarily *its* first in a sequence); the coefficient is not significant in either equation, but it suggests that subsequent downsizings yield 1–2 percent higher excess returns.[53]

2. A variable that we collected but did not so far employ is the length of the time period over which the announced downsizing was projected to occur. On the assumption of convex adjustment costs a given downsizing (L) should have a stronger negative effect the shorter the time horizon over which it is implemented. We assumed that this duration is a decision variable for the firm chosen to minimize the adjustment cost of the necessary layoffs, but subject to the consideration that dire circumstances might compel swifter action. Therefore we regressed the length of the announced downsizing period on the (absolute) number of employees to be laid off (with 421 observations the t-statistic = 7.91). We entered the residual as an exogenous variable in the model, expecting a positive coefficient (i.e., a hasty downsizing elicits a more negative market reaction). The coefficient is indeed positive but only weakly significant ($t = 1.54$).

3. A question sometimes treated in event studies is whether different or more predictable market reactions occur when more information is announced (indicated by the length of the *Wall Street Journal* story). Brickley and Van Drunen found much more statistical significance in reactions to stories longer than the median in their sample. Our results are different. When the sample is split around the median-length story, a somewhat better fit is actually preserved for the short than for the

long stories. Story length is correlated with company size (it was not, for Brickley and Van Drunen), and splitting the sample around median company size yields a parallel result: better explanatory power for small firms. The concern that these findings might arouse is greatly reduced by the results of Table 2.9 (*SGA* is uncorrelated with company size).

4. Could we have obscured important behavior by summing excess returns over the *Wall Street Journal* publication date and the two days preceding it? We replaced the three-day return by the individual-day returns and re-estimated the model. The models for days XR0 and XRM2 closely resemble the three-day model, but that for XRM1 (the day on which many of the announcements were first made public) is somewhat different. The dummy indicating an announced reorganization is significantly positive, but the fraction laid off and the dummy for white-collar discharges are not significant.

5. The automobile industry was a conspicuous downsizer during 1987- 1991, the source of no less than 63 of our 513 announcements. Because some of these represent the routinized temporary plant closings that are common in the auto industry, we were concerned that these observations might somehow be distorting our regression results. Fortunately, when the auto-company observations are deleted the basic model (Table 2.8) is essentially unchanged. This industry's distinctive pattern did, however, account for our early decision to drop the dummy for temporary closings from the analysis.

In conclusion, with the qualification that some levels of statistical significance are marginal, we find that the data consistently support the hypothesis developed previously in the paper: one cannot rule out the hypothesis that nonproduction-worker cadres are overinflated in successful corporations, necessitating negative shocks to trigger a value-increasing reorganization. This analysis is just the first step of investigating the situations of these downsizing companies. We hope to proceed to track their situations back in time, taking account of their market-structure environments and governance situations, to ascertain what circumstances brought them to the point where a substantial reduction in the resources that they employed was mandated.

2.7. SUMMARY AND CONCLUSIONS

The large reductions of white-collar employment in major U.S. companies during the past decade or so raise the question of why this apparent "fat" could accumulate and what shocks promote its removal. The question is underlined by various results of scholarly research, such as the negative association of an industry's plants' productive efficiency with the prevalence of "inbound" diversification and the productivity gains associated with changes in corporate control and with corporate "refocusing" strategies during the 1980s. Cadres of nonproduction employees could be inflated by various mechanisms, including managerial preferences in firms poorly monitored by their shareholders. The mechanism on which we focus is Niskanen's version of the lateral contract within a firm that employs diverse groups of nonproduction workers as functional specialists. This mechanism yields predictions about both where (and when) the inflation of white-collar employment should occur and what sorts of disturbance would excise it.

We investigated whether the nonproduction labor used by three-digit U.S. manufacturing industries was reduced by competitive disturbances in their product markets (increases in imports' market share) and in the market for corporate control (turnover of assets in their industry through related and unrelated mergers). Import competition exerted this effect significantly, to a degree that increased through the 1970s to a high level in the 1980s. The story is more complex for changes in control. Consistent with the conventional wisdom, unrelated acquisitions tended to inflate white-collar employment in the 1970s but had the reverse effect in the 1980s. Related acquisitions, more likely to involve the transfer of business assets into hands that can utilize them better, tend if anything to be associated with increased nonproduction employment. The analysis was applied to total nonproduction employees located at manufacturing establishments and at central offices and other administrative establishments, and to plant-based nonproduction workers separately. In general the results indicate that employees in administrative establishments are more vulnerable to fat-excising shocks (especially in the 1980s), but differences in the results between nonproduction-worker counts excluding and including the administrative establishments (and irregularities in data for the latter) are cautionary. Another major qualification is that we do not control for hypotheses about sources of downsizing based on value-maximizing responses to disturbances. Possible examples of these are changes in the technology of organization or in the feasibility of contracting out white-collar tasks formerly performed in-house.

If these adverse shocks forced profit-increasing white-collar lay-offs on some firms, the stock market should have reacted positively to some layoff announcements, and so we analyzed stock-market reactions to announcements of corporate downsizings made during 1987-1991. Two factors could affect the market's reactions to these downsizings: the negative information effect of the bad news that the announcement reveals to shareholders; and the positive reaction of informed shareholders who welcome an indication of decisive action against corporate inefficiency. The mean excess returns are significantly negative though with a large minority of positive reactions. The associations between the excess returns and traits of the announcement imply that reactions to the announcements reflect a mixture of "bad news" and "bite the bullet" components. In particular, market valuations of downsizing announcements tend to be positive when white-collar discharges are involved, an effect strengthened when a reorganization is also announced. Plant closures also offset the negative effect of layoffs.

The analytical perspective of this paper suggests that the risk of corporate obesity is greatest when the firm is successful and when its industrial base mandates extensive reliance on the services of diverse nonproduction workers. We got rather indecisive results in testing whether the downsizing effects of adverse shocks varies with industries' market-structure traits. However, when firms were sorted by the importance of their overhead-intensities per employee, it turned out that the stock market's reaction to downsizing announcements is strongly predictable in high-overhead firms, unpredictable in low-overhead firms.

This finding about efficiency and overhead intensity is important for relating our analysis to the views on efficiency and corporate governance that are standard in the finance literature.[54] The two approaches are complementary and broadly consistent, but there might be an important difference in their policy implications. The finance literature concludes (to put it crudely) that there is nothing wrong with U.S. industry that an orgy of hostile takeovers can't fix. Our findings raise the possibility that the efficiency level which optimal boardroom arrangements can achieve is importantly qualified by bureaucratic dynamics in the internal organization of large, successful firms engaged in complex tasks.

NOTES

1. We use the term "white-collar" synonymously with nonproduction labor, the empirical focus of this paper, although they are not exactly congruent.

2. *Wall Street Journal*, July 25, 1986, p. B1; Shleifer and Summers (1988).

3. Bureau of Labor Statistics data quoted in *Business Week*, October 1, 1990, pp. 130-131.

4. See Hammer and Champy (1993).

5. Berman, Bound, and Griliches (1993). Notice that their analysis dealt with employment in manufacturing establishments and not with administrative and related establishments, which house an increasing proportion of nonproduction employees.

6. The change in the classification system for occupations and its consequences for comparability over time are described in U.S. Bureau of the Census (1989). Our method of reclassifying 1970 employment to the revised 1980 categories was suggested in correspondence by Thomas S. Schopp. The comparison of 1970 and 1980 employment by industry is further complicated by the change in the Standard Industrial Classification in 1972, which rendered some industries noncomparable between 1970 and 1980.

7. For real-output changes we relied on the data base that supports the Department of Commerce's annual *U.S. Industrial Outlook*. See U.S. Bureau of Industrial Economics (1983), pp. A-2 to A-19.

8. Figures quoted in *Business Week*, October 1, 1990, p. 130.

9. These data are taken from U.S. Bureau of Labor Statistics (1991a), Table 5. Also see Herz (1990), Table 11, where data for workers re-employed in January 1988 are supplied for more industries. The proportion reporting

lower earnings was 44.6 percent for all manufacturing, 46.2 percent for durable goods, 63.5 percent for primary metals, 50.5 percent for fabricated metal products, 43.7 percent for nonelectrical machinery, 30 percent for electrical machinery, 50 percent for automobiles, and 62.7 percent for other transportation equipment.

10. See Herz (1990). From the surveys of displaced workers Farber (1993) developed various conclusions that are complementary to these. He found higher rates of job loss for older and better educated workers in 1990-91 than during the 1980s, and the difference is not associated with a rate of plant closings higher than in earlier years. He does question whether older and better educated workers who were displaced recently suffered a significant decrease in the probability of obtaining a new job.

11. Bureau of Labor Statistics data quoted *Wall Street Journal*, July 25, 1986, p. B1.

12. *Wall Street Journal*, April 5, 1990, pp. B1, B6.

13. See Alchian and Demsetz (1972), Holmstrom (1982), and Holmstrom and Tirole (1989). Winter proposed that the firm's administrative cadre is importantly engaged in producing "unconventional assets" that are not specifically observable outside the firm and unnecessary to current production, but do sustain the continuation value of the firm in the long run. Inputs to this production process is indistinguishable from inputs that represent pure fat. See Sidney G. Winter, "Routines, Cash Flows, and Unconventional Assets: Corporate Change in the 1980s," in Blair (1993), pp. 55-97.

14. See the literature survey of Sumanth, Omachonu, and Beruvides (1990) and the papers contained in Lehrer (1983).

15. See Williamson (1963).

16. See Cyert and March (1963).

17. This point was developed extensively by Nelson and Winter (1982, chap. 5). Notice the consistency between this approach and the hypothesis that the marginal products of most white-collar staff are effectively unobservable.

18. See Niskanen (1971).

19. For example, *Wall Street Journal*, July 23, 1992, pp. A1, A5, October 1, 1992, pp. A1, A12; *Business Week*, December 23, 1991, p. 27.

20. See Dertouzos, Lester, and Solow (1989), chapter 7. Evidence also appears in case studies such as Rayner (1975).

21. Nickell, Wadhwani, and Wall (1991) and also Geroski (1989).

22. See Caves and Barton (1990), pp. 91, 96-99, 127-128. The data did not permit identifying the diversified plants of multi-industry firms as the specific culprits, but it did allow localizing the inefficiency to each industry's

larger plants, in which these should be overrepresented. Among the many other influences controlled was oligopolistic behavior, which indeed reduces efficiency where levels of seller concentration are moderate or higher. The test of corporate diversification's effect could not be replicated exactly on other industrial countries, but the relationship appears unique to the United States; see Caves and Associates (1992, chap. 1).

23. See Lichtenberg and Siegel (1990). The proportion of nonproduction employees working in administrative establishments rose from 2.8 percent in 1954 to 6.7 percent in 1982 (*1982 Census of Manufactures*, Vol. 1, Introduction, p. xx).

24. We decided to forswear undertaking any analysis of the determinants of changes of employment in administrative establishments alone, because of the noisiness of the data and possible biases due to substitutability between nonproduction workers at plant locations and at administrative establishments. It would be desirable to analyze the determinants of changes in administrative establishments' employment, but only with access to establishment data, as an extension of Lichtenberg and Siegel (1990). We shall, however, draw some tentative conclusions about administrative establishments from differences in the determinants of changes in plant-based and total nonproduction employment.

25. See Hamermesh (1986). Berman, Bound, and Griliches (1993) omitted wage variables from their similar cross-section analysis on the ground that sectoral wage variations are likely to be endogenous. We include them partly because our analysis has a time-series dimension, partly because we are concerned not with unbiased estimates of wage effects but with the omission of substantial influences on nonproduction-worker employment.

26. See Freeman and Medoff (1982).

27. See Berndt, Morrison, and Rosenblum (1992), Berman, Bound, and Griliches (1993), and Brynjolfsson and Hitt (1993).

28. Somewhat similar functions were estimated for production and nonproduction employees separately in a study using a panel of annual data 1970-1979 for Canadian manufacturing industries (Caves, 1990). It was found that the nonproduction-worker and production-worker demand models behave rather similarly, and tariff reductions induced cuts in the use of both types of labor. For nonproduction labor, however, the great bulk of the variance in the panel data was interindustry and not intertemporal, and increases in real output in the 1970s typically involved little if any expansion of nonproduction employment.

29. See Ravenscraft and Scherer (1987).

30. Lichtenberg and Siegel (1990). Lichtenberg and Siegel (1987) found that control changes on average are productive when observed across the board for all manufacturing establishments. Baldwin and Caves (1991) obtained the same result for Canada, but associated the productivity gains from control changes not with reduced labor inputs (nonproduction or other) but with the redeployment of intangible assets. We conjecture that the difference between the U.S. and Canadian results is due to the focus of Lichtenberg and Siegel (1990) on auxiliary establishments belonging to large enterprises, whereas the Canadian analysis covered all establishments and embraced few large and diversified independent enterprises.

31. See Bhagat, Shleifer, and Vishny (1990) and Healy, Palepu, and Ruback (1992).

32. In assembling a similar data base Blair, Lane, and Schary (1991) made the distressing discovery that the overlap between the 1979 transactions identified by the FTC and in the ADP data base is only half of the FTC total count and one-fifth of the ADP total.

33. See Pugel (1980). Domowitz, Hubbard, and Petersen (1986) found that increased import competition was one source of the collapse in the 1970s of the (cross-section) relation between price-cost margins and concentration in U.S. manufacturing.

34. See Bloch (1974).

35. See Caves and Associates (1992).

36. See Caves (1988). Long ago Delehanty (1968) observed positive correlations between these structural attributes of industries and their proportions of nonproduction employees.

37. See Katz and Murphy (1992), Murphy and Welch (1991), and Revenga (1992).

38. An instrumental-variables approach might work if the data set were expanded from quinquennial to annual changes, but the quinquennial changes accord with both the available data and the putatively slow working of disturbances from import competition and corporate-control changes.

39. The denominator of WDIFR is always average annual compensation per production worker in manufacturing establishments. The numerator is either a weighted average of average annual compensation in administrative and production establishments or the average for nonproduction workers in production establishments only. Incidentally, we noticed that (as expected) the compensation of nonproduction workers in manufacturing and administrative units is strongly correlated among industries, and that auxiliary-establishment

compensation is typically a little higher than in the same industry's manufacturing plants.

40. Margaret M. Blair and Martha A. Schary, "Industry-Level Pressures to Restructure," in Blair (1993), pp. 149-203.

41. Compared to 1967-1972 the standard deviation of WDIFR indeed increased in 1972-1982 by one-third for all nonproduction employees and by nearly one-half for those in manufacturing plants. However, in 1982-1986 it rose by one-fourth more in both groups.

42. The coefficient's magnitude implies that when 5 percent of an industry's assets change hands in related mergers during a five-year period (roughly the sample mean) its nonproduction employment falls by nearly 1 percent.

43. The coefficient for NPRA in 1982-86 implies that the turnover of 5 percent of an industry's assets in a five-year period would lead to a 12 percent reduction in nonproduction employment. The figure is non-credibly high, especially in light of other coefficients on unrelated mergers, but it does suggest a substantial effect.

44. See MacDonald (1992).

45. See Scherer and Huh (1992).

46. One can think of exceptions, such as when the demand curve is rendered less elastic, but overall the assumption seems reasonable.

47. Analyses of cases of financial distress indicate that they provide an occasion for managers to reverse committed policies of the firm that have proven unsuccessful. See Wruck (1990) and Shefrin and Statman (1986).

48. Blackwell, Marr, and Spivey (1990) investigated the bad-news effect in a sample of announcements of permanent plant-closings. They observed significant negative excess returns, and the firms' accounting returns on equity had underperformed their three-digit SIC industries in the preceding two years. Worrell, Davidson, and Sharma (1991) also reported significant negative market reactions to announcements of layoffs.

49. Excess returns on other trading days are insignificant and do not warrant attention (the positive value for XRP1 is strongly influenced by one huge outlier).

50. It is based on 512 observations because of one missing excess-return value.

51. Worrell, Davidson, and Sharma reported that excess returns due to layoff announcements were not significantly different from zero when reorganization and consolidation were also announced, significantly negative (-2.46 percent) when the layoffs occurred simply because the firm was running losses. Statman and Sepe observed positive excess returns to announcements of

project terminations in cases where shareholders already had information on the project's prospects for success.

52. Brickley and Van Drunen (1990) analyzed market valuations of announcements of internal corporate reorganizations, finding significant positive returns (for the more conspicuous events) of 0.7 to 1.15 percent. The small size of the gain might reflect (they note) the fact that the reorganizations commonly affect only a division or other small proportion of a company. In general they found that liquidations of divisions or subsidiaries get negative market reactions, other reorganizations positive reactions. They also observed that firms reorganizing in order to increase efficiency or cut costs had previously exhibited stock-market performance worse than their industry, consistent with the bite-the-bullet hypothesis of our own study.

53. A sufficient reason for the insignificance of this dummy is that our hypotheses embrace expectations of both positive and negative excess returns. If the market values a strategic change chiefly upon its first announcement, the announcement of subsequent steps will tend to bring reactions that are smaller in absolute but not in algebraic value. The force of this consideration is seen when we regress the squared value of three-day excess returns on the variable indicating subsequent announcements: the coefficient is negative, with $t = 2.97$.

54. Jensen (1993) provides a forceful statement.

III

Incomplete Contracting and Costly Disclosure: A Study of Strategic Preannouncement of Layoffs

3.1. INTRODUCTION

The phenomenon of corporate layoffs has received a considerable amount of attention in recent years. Likewise, there has been a proliferation of event studies analyzing the announcement of layoffs. The temporal relationship between the announcement and execution of layoffs, however, has been largely ignored. This lack of scholarly attention is perhaps attributable to the traditional perspective of looking exclusively at product market explanations of product market actions. The manager's problem of deciding when optimally to announce a layoff, given that the implementation schedule for the layoff has been determined, is a trivial one from the narrow product market perspective. This is because management scholars have amassed an impressive body of case study and survey evidence indicating that managers believe preannouncing layoffs adversely affects worker productivity.[1] This belief, regardless of the actual productivity implications of preannouncement (which are arguably very difficult to measure), is sufficient to render the question of optimal layoff timing moot from a narrow product market perspective. Intended profit-maximizing managers will always seek to minimize the time between layoff announcement and the physical departure of the terminated employees.

Although the theoretical justifications offered for minimizing announcement lead times are numerous and compelling,[2] these arguments are difficult to reconcile with the distribution of layoff announcement lead times (defined as the time between the announcement date and the projected layoff completion date) observed for the sample of all layoff announcements which appeared in the Wall Street Journal from 1987-1991 that specifically mention the planned implementation period.

Announcement Lead Time (months)	Number of Observations
0< Lead time <= 1	194
1< Lead time <= 3	109
3< Lead time <= 6	43
6< Lead time <= 12	34
12< Lead time	41

The modal lead time of less than one month is consistent with managers' stated beliefs that preannouncement lowers worker productivity; however, a significant minority of layoffs are stretched out over periods longer than one year. If managers believe that layoff preannouncements adversely affect worker productivity, profit maximizing managers should never preannounce layoffs unless there is some offsetting benefit to doing so. The purpose of this paper is to suggest that it may be necessary to look beyond the product market to find this offsetting benefit.

It is possible that this offsetting benefit can be found in the linkage between product markets and capital markets. In fact, the purpose of this paper is to suggest that layoff preannouncements cannot be fully understood without reference to this linkage. Notably, of the 41 announcements with lead times exceeding one year, roughly 40% occurred immediately prior to major borrowing efforts by the announcer or one of its product market rivals (the terms 'major' and 'immediately prior' will be made precise below). This finding is especially interesting in light of the fact that only 10% of all layoff announcements immediately preceded such activity. The potential strategic significance of this contemporaneous timing is that Moody's and Standard and Poor's often mention announced cost-cutting efforts as reasons for upgrading a firm's credit rating, even before implementation commences.[3] The temporal proximity of layoff announcements to rival borrowing may have similar strategic significance, as suggested by anecdotal evidence gathered during interviews with investment bankers who indicated that it is not unusual for road shows (i.e. series of presentations undertaken with the express intention of generating interest in a securities offering) to be postponed in response to negative industry news announced by other firms in the same industry.

This paper, which is similar in spirit to recent work in the industrial organization literature on the linkages between product markets and capital markets, exploits the fact that product market decisions and financing decisions are not independent. Chevalier (1995) and Bolton and Scharfstein (1990) demonstrate that external financing constraints, long heralded as a solution to the agency costs arising from imperfect governance structures, can alter behavior in product markets. By presenting empirical evidence that an important motivation for early announcements of layoffs is to alter the cost of raising capital, either for the announcing firm or its rivals, this paper suggests that causation can also flow the other way: product market actions can influence external financing constraints. The methodological approach employed herein is to exploit the fact that layoff announcements are voluntary disclosures which are costly to the firm. As such they may be useful as self-commitment devices when managers are unable contractually to commit to future layoffs.

Section 3.2 of this paper describes why managers are unable to write contracts with their creditors regarding future layoffs and may therefore be forced to rely on costly preannouncements in order to influence near-term capital costs. Section 3.3 describes more formally the information asymmetries that could make layoff preannouncement a profitable way to raise rivals' borrowing costs or lower one's own. Testable implications of the models are then discussed. Section 3.4 describes the data, selection of the sample, and classification of announcements as strategic or non-strategic. Section 3.5 contains empirical evidence. Section 3.6 concludes and presents suggestions for future research.

3.2. INCOMPLETE CONTRACTING AND THE VALUE OF COSTLY DISCLOSURE

If a firm's prospective creditors believe that the firm's employment level exceeds the optimum, it is in the firm's interest to persuade these creditors before borrowing that the problem will be redressed. Similarly, if the prospective creditors of a firm's rival believe that the future of the industry looks rosy, it is in the firm's interest to persuade the rival's creditors that this optimistic forecast is unfounded. In either case, a credible commitment to undertake a sizable layoff will serve the intended purpose. Of course, if the firm could execute the layoffs prior to its own debt offer date (or its rival's announced offer date), credible commitments would be unnecessary. One can easily imagine, however, instances in which the firm's managers recognize the excessiveness of their work force but do not yet know exactly which employees should be fired. If investigation of the firm's nonoptimality is subject to what Dierickx and Cool (1989) refer to as time compression diseconomies (i.e. adjustment costs that are convex with respect to time), credible commitments to undertake the needed layoff in the future may be valuable in the presence of near-term capital market activity.

Given that managers believe the public preannouncement of layoffs adversely affects productivity, the first-best solution would be to convey privately to the firm's prospective creditors (or its rival's prospective creditors) that the firm intends to undertake a major layoff. Unfortunately for the managers, mere promises concerning future layoffs will not be credible if creditors assume that the managers suffer disutility from firing workers.

If contracting costs are positive, but not prohibitive, the second-best solution would be for the manager to commit contractually to future layoffs. In this way, the promise to reduce employment in the future is made credible and public preannouncement, with its attendant productivity costs, is avoided. The problem with this approach is that in the real world the cost of writing contracts that dictate future employment levels is prohibitive as seen from the creditor's perspective.

One of the fundamental precepts of lender liability law is that a firm's creditors must not unduly interfere in the day-to-day operations of the firm. While creditors commonly attach covenants to loan agreements based on various financial indicators of the firm's health, it is exceedingly rare to attach covenants based on operating indicators like employee headcount. The reason that lenders are loathe to write covenants on operating indicators, according to corporate attorneys we interviewed, is that the lender, if it is deemed to have interfered with management, can be held responsible for all of the firm's debts in the event of insolvency, not just the money owed to the lender in question.[4]

Given that the first-best option of promising layoffs is not credible, and the option of contractual commitment is deemed prohibitively expensive, public preannouncement of a layoff may be the least cost means of credibly committing to reduce future employment.

Public preannouncements of impending layoffs should serve as credible commitments to reduce employment because of what Farrell and Gibbons (1989) refer to as *mutual discipline*. Managers would like to overstate layoffs to the capital markets in order to raise rivals' costs or lower their own; however, the penalty for doing so within earshot of the firm's own workers is a greater loss in productivity. It is the mutual discipline imposed by the existence of the firm's employees as a second audience that makes the layoff claims credible. Since the incentives to lie work in opposite directions, public claims may be credible even when claims made privately to creditors or workers are not.[5] In fact, there is considerable evidence that suggests layoff announcements are deemed credible commitments to reduce employment. As noted above, Moody's and Standard and Poor's have mentioned announced cost-cutting efforts as reasons for upgrading a firm's credit rating. Also, the stated justification for some layoff preannouncements is the protection of the announcing firm's existing credit rating.[6] Thus, the mutual discipline enforced by managers' countervailing incentives to lie when simultaneously communicating with creditors and workers may enable the firm to lower its borrowing costs or raise its rival's.

Once a major layoff is announced, the firm pays a penalty in the form of reduced worker productivity. As a result, however, the firm may be able to obtain needed funds immediately at better terms than would have been available absent the commitment to reduce employment. This will be true if the capital markets are aware of the firm's excess employment and it is less costly in terms of lost productivity to announce the optimal layoff before borrowing than it is to postpone the borrowing until the optimal layoff is completed. Similarly, the firm may also find it profitable to strategically preannounce a layoff upon discovering its rival's intention to borrow in the near future.

Layoff preannouncements may raise rivals' capital costs by revealing managers' private assessments about their industry's outlook. In other words, layoff announcements may be a means of disclosing to the capital markets that the announcing firm's future does not look rosy. If future states of the world in which optimal employment is lower are positively correlated with states of the world in which expected profits are lower[7], and the firm's managers have better information about their company's future than the capital markets, layoff announcements should induce potential lenders to reassess the credit worthiness of the announcing firm. If the announcing firm does not anticipate borrowing in the immediate future, this reassessment should be a matter of little concern.

A more interesting point is that this reassessment may also apply to other firms in the same industry. To the extent that participants in the same industry have correlated types, the announcing firm is also revealing information about its rivals' types. The central tenet of the literature on strategic groups is that close product market rivals are similarly affected by common external disturbances.[8] Also, empirical studies such as Schmalensee's (1985) decomposition of the variance in firm profitability into components attributable to firm, industry, and market share effects suggests that industry effects are of paramount importance.[9] The correlation of types therefore suggests one way in which preannouncing bad news may be beneficial to the announcer. If a firm is aware that its rival is about to go to the capital markets for a large sum of money, the strategic timing of negative industry news may raise the cost of funds incurred by the rival. In order for layoff preannouncements to raise rivals' borrowing costs, it is necessary that the support of the capital markets' prior distribution function on future industry profitability include values which, under complete information, would lead to different borrowing costs for the rival. This condition seems to hold given the aforementioned evidence that it is not unusual for a road show to be postponed in response to negative industry news announced by other firms in the same industry.

It is important to note that as long as the capital market's perceptions about the firm's optimal employment level are correct, neither the firm's desire to lower its capital costs nor the desire to raise its rivals' necessarily implies that workers will be fired solely for information-related reasons (although this is certainly not precluded). Only the timing of the layoff announcement need be affected by strategic information-revelation considerations.

3.3. COSTLY DISCLOSURE MODEL AND TESTABLE IMPLICATIONS

The costly disclosure model developed in this section describes more formally how strategic considerations may impinge on announcement timing decisions.[10] Strategic behavior models generally involve an information asymmetry in which one player is uncertain about another player's type and a conjunction of structural conditions that create the opportunity for players of one type to profitably distinguish themselves. The cases developed below are driven by the capital markets' uncertainty about the probability that a layoff will occur. Borrowing activity by a firm or its rival creates the opportunity for managers to profitably resolve this uncertainty. The type of self-commitment undertaken by the announcing firm is the same in each case; only the structural context differs.

The case in which managers seek to raise their rivals' borrowing costs by forcing lenders to reassess the rivals' credit worthiness is labeled the *bad news* case. The bad news case is similar in spirit to a number of signaling models in the predation literature which involve a firm attempting to convince its rival that the rival faces a grim future in the industry.[11]

The case in which managers seek to lower their firm's own borrowing costs by revealing their intention to redress the firm's employment problem, labeled *bite-the-bullet*, is presented next. The bite-the-bullet case differs from the bad news case in that the structural conditions that make disclosure profitable lie in the threats and opportunities impinging on a single firm, mediated by the organizational technology of the firm's efficient response to them. Testable hypotheses which devolve from these cases are then discussed.

Case 1: Bad News

	Optimal Strategic Announcement Date		Optimal Non-Strategic Announcement Date	
_____T_0_____	_____X_1__T_1_		_____X_2__T_2____
Industry Decline Revealed to Mgrs But Not Cap Mkts.	Optimal Debt Offer Date For Rival		Optimal Layoff Conclusion Date

At exogenously determined time T_0, managers become aware that the industry is facing a market-wide disturbance that lowers optimal quantity and that maximizing firm value requires a reduction in the size of the firm's work force. Managers, who do not know exactly whom to fire, begin investigating the firm's nonoptimality at T_0 in order to determine precisely which employees should be fired. Neither the capital markets nor the firm's employees have any knowledge of the impending layoffs until management announces a specific layoff target or begins firing people without announcing a target.

The point at which management knows exactly whom to fire, T_2, is technologically determined given T_0 by assuming that speeding up the layoff generates cost convexities and that delaying the layoffs past the point of discovery also generates cost convexities. These are fairly standard assumptions about organizational technology.[12] One mechanism that generates such convexities is provided by Keren and Levhari (1983). In their model, the firm's external operating environment, and therefore its optimal production plan, changes at discrete intervals. They derive the optimal implementation time for a new production plan by weighing the time-dependent costs of developing a new plan against the flow costs of operating with the existing inefficient plan.

If strategic disclosure concerns are unimportant, managers will delay the layoff announcement until they have nearly full knowledge of whom to fire because the per period losses in productivity due to pre-announcement are assumed to be large relative to the per period losses from retaining workers whose wages exceed their marginal products. This seems reasonable because presumably only a subset of the firm's work force is overpaid while the specter of massive layoffs may affect the productivity of the firm's entire work force. As a result, the lead time will be as short as possible in the absence of borrowing.[13] Thus, the optimal non-strategic announcement date, X_2, is also technologically determined given the information revealed about the excessiveness of the firm's work force at T_0.

T_1 is the exogenously determined (at least from the announcer's perspective) date at which the firm's industry rival has announced it will borrow a large amount of capital. Managers of the firm investigating their own nonoptimality learn the rival's optimal borrowing date at some point prior to T_1 (possibly before T_0). This knowledge is transmitted because the rival must publicize its intent to borrow in order to generate interest in its debt offering.

T_1 may occur anywhere on the timeline, but the interesting case from the perspective of analyzing strategic preannouncement is where T_1 occurs in the interval between T_0 and X_2. If T_1 occurs before T_0, there is no opportunity for strategic disclosure. Likewise, if T_1 occurs after X_2, there is no information asymmetry because, even in the absence of strategic considerations, the announcement occurs at X_2. If, however, T_1 occurs in the interval between T_0 and X_2, strategic preannouncement of layoffs may arise as a profitable form of self-commitment even though the optimal layoff plan is not yet in place. The manager's costly disclosure of private information may raise the rival's borrowing costs more than enough to compensate the firm for the productivity losses engendered by preannouncement. The rational-

ity constraint faced by a manager considering strategic preannouncement to raise rivals' borrowing costs takes the form:

$ of productivity loss due to preannouncement	<	$ of profit gain due to rival's market contraction induced by increased unit costs

If the firms compete à la Cournot, the rival's increased borrowing
costs result in higher unit costs which cause the rival's reaction function to shift inward leading the rival to contract. While the announcing
firm may profit from this contraction, the effect on the rival's capital
costs must be substantial because the announcing firm's productivity
loss (and the resulting inward shift of its own reaction function) is first
order while its profit gain in the product market is second order[14].

If the rationality constraint is satisfied, managers who know that
layoffs are needed but lack the detailed knowledge necessary to implement them immediately may find it optimal to preannounce the bad
news prior to the rival's borrowing date.

Case 2: Bite-the-Bullet

	Optimal Strategic Announcement Date	Optimal Non-Strategic Announcement Date
___ T_0 ___	___ X_1 ___ T_1 ___	___ X_2 ___ T_2 ___
Firm Nonoptimality Revealed to Mgrs and Cap Mkts.	Optimal Debt Offer Date	Optimal Layoff Conclusion Date

The primary feature which distinguishes the bite-the-bullet case
from the bad news case is the nature of the information asymmetry
between managers and the capital markets. In this case the capital market is aware that the firm has excess employment but is uncertain
whether the problem will be redressed. One possible reason for this
uncertainty involves differences among managers in the layoff execution date. Good managers are those who recognize the problem and
take the optimal action at the optimal time. Bad managers continue

operating with the inefficient plan beyond the firm's optimal layoff conclusion date.[15]

At exogenously-determined time T_0, managers and the capital markets become aware that maximizing firm value requires a reduction in the size of the firm's work force. Neither managers nor capital markets know exactly whom to fire at T_0. Negative earnings, stock price declines, and the like are all fairly cogent indicators of some type of nonoptimality; however, it is quite another matter to know precisely which employees should be fired. As before, managers begin investigating the firm's nonoptimality at T_0. The optimal layoff conclusion date (T_2) and the optimal non-strategic announcement date (X_2) are technologically determined as before.

T_1 is the exogenously determined date at which the firm needs to borrow a large amount of capital.[16] Managers learn the optimal borrowing date at some point prior to T_1 (possibly before T_0), but T_1 is assumed to be economically unalterable.[17] As before, T_1 may occur anywhere on the timeline, but the interesting case is where T_1 occurs in the interval between T_0 and X_2. If T_1 occurs before T_0 or after X_2, there is no information asymmetry between managers and the capital markets and therefore nothing to signal. Nobody is aware of the firm's nonoptimality prior to T_0 and there is no private information about the manager's type after X_2 because good managers announced a layoff at X_2.

If, however, T_1 occurs in the interval between T_0 and X_2, strategic preannouncement of layoffs may arise as a profitable form of self-commitment even though the optimal layoff plan is not yet in place. The capital markets know the firm has too many workers, but the manager's type is unknown. Therefore the capital markets are not certain the problem will be redressed at the optimal time. Announcing a layoff prior to T_1 allows good managers to distinguish themselves from bad managers if:

Productivity losses given optimal layoff date	< prospective interest cost reductions	< Productivity losses given bad manager's layoff date

Whatever the announcement date, productivity losses will persist for a longer period of time if the manager is a bad manager because bad managers prefer a later layoff conclusion date. The capital market's beliefs about the probability that managers will resolve the firm's employment problem by the optimal layoff conclusion date are a function of the severity of the problem. This is equivalent to assuming that the ability of bad managers to postpone layoffs is constrained by the degree of nonoptimality revealed at T_0. The capital markets' beliefs, based on publicly observable information, take the form:

P(managers fire workers) = F(lagged operating ratios, lagged stock
                                           price performance, etc.)

Testable Implications of the Models

If the assumptions underlying the signaling models developed above accurately depict reality and capital market signaling considerations are important, a number of empirical implications follow.

First, layoff announcements which immediately precede borrowing by a firm or its rivals (hereafter referred to as "strategic" layoff announcements) should, on average, have longer lead times than announcements which do not precede borrowing.[18] This can be seen in Figure 3.1 which shows the optimal lead time as a function of the optimal borrowing date, for a layoff of a given size (i.e. controlling for adjustment costs). The horizontal axis recreates the timelines from the previous section. The location of the optimal borrowing date (T_1) on the timeline determines the optimal layoff announcement date. Since the optimal layoff conclusion date (T_2) is technologically determined, T_1 is sufficient to calculate the optimal lead time given T_0. If T_1 occurs outside the interval T_0X_2, the lead time will be as short as possible subject to adjustment costs. This interval is labeled "optimal nonstrategic lead time". Within the interval T_0X_2, the optimal strategic lead time increases in lockstep with increases in the time between T_1 and X_2. In this interval, layoff announcements will immediately precede the optimal borrowing date. Thus, if strategic disclosure is an important determinant of preannouncements:

Figure 3.1
Hypothesized Differences Between Strategic and Non-Strategic Lead Times

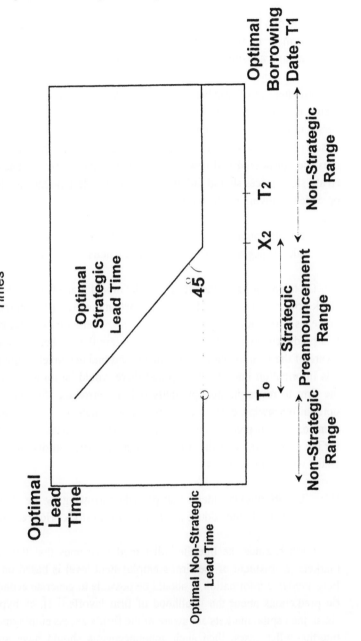

H1:   Layoffs that immediately precede trips to the capital market by a firm or its rivals should be announced further in advance than layoffs not subject to strategic informational considerations.

Another set of testable hypotheses that devolves from the asymmetric information model concerns the stock price reactions to strategic versus non-strategic announcements. In order for preannouncements to raise rivals' costs of borrowing, the strategic layoff announcements must be considered bad news by the rivals' shareholders.[19] Therefore rivals' stock prices should fall in response to layoff announcements that precede borrowing by the rivals.[20]

H2:   Layoff announcements that precede borrowing by rivals should adduce negative rival stock price reactions.

On the other hand, the bite-the-bullet model predicts that own firm stock price reactions should be positive when the layoff announcement precedes borrowing by the announcing firm. There are two reasons for this predicted favorable reaction. First, unless the market was already aware of the firm's excess employment (and had negatively capitalized this information into the stock price) there would be no incentive for the firm to reveal its nonoptimality before borrowing. Second, if the optimal borrowing date precedes the optimal non-strategic announcement date, then preannouncement reveals that the manager's concern for the present value of the firm outweighs the personal disutility associated with firing workers.

H3:   Layoff announcements that precede borrowing by the announcing firm should adduce positive own firm stock price reactions.

Further, since the bite-the-bullet model assumes that the capital markets' assessment of the firm's employment level is based on publicly available information, it should be possible to generate econometric predictions about the likelihood of firm layoffs.[21] If, as hypothesized, the capital markets are aware of the firm's excess employment in bite-the-bullet cases, then such announcements should have significantly higher predicted layoff probabilities than the remainder of the sample. This is because the remaining announcements presumably reflect some mixture of bite-the-bullet and bad news type effects. Some non-strategic announcements will be anticipated by the capital markets, some will not. A number of layoff event studies confirm the cross-sectional heterogeneity of stock market responses to layoff announcements.[22]

H4:   In an empirical estimation of layoff probabilities based on observable firm characteristics, layoff announcements that precede borrowing by announcing firms should have higher predicted layoff probabilities than announcements that do not.

Finally, if preannouncements are truly used as a form of costly disclosure, bluffing should not occur. Specifically, the difference between announced and realized employment reductions should be no greater when strategic incentives to preannounce are present than when they are absent. The premise upon which this paper is built is that layoff announcements are not cheap talk.[23]

H5:   The difference between announced and actual work force reductions should be no greater in the presence of strategic considerations than in their absence.

3.4. SAMPLE SELECTION, DATA, AND ANNOUNCEMENT CLASSIFICATION

Sample Selection and Data

The sample used to examine empirically the hypotheses formulated in Section 3.3 consists of all layoffs announced in the Wall Street Journal during the years 1987-1991. Since the core hypotheses concern the impact of strategic considerations on lead times, announcements which do not specifically mention the time horizon over which the layoff is to be implemented were excluded.[24] Financial firms were also removed from the sample due to the difficulty of linking borrowing by financial firms to activity in a particular product market. The sample was further narrowed to include only firms for which stock price data was available from the Center for Research in Securities Prices (CRSP). The final sample consists of 330 layoff announcements. The distribution of announcements across two digit SIC codes for industry groups that accounted for at least five sample announcements is shown in Table 3.1.

In order to identify situations in which the strategic preannouncement of layoffs may have been profitably exploited to influence capital costs, we collected information on the borrowing activity of the 330 announcers and their three to five largest rivals during the sample period from the Securities Data Corporation. All instances in which a sample firm borrowed at least $200 million in a single offering were recorded. The debt offering information encompasses: the filing dates and offer dates for all non-shelf issues of at least $200 million, the offer dates for Regulation D (Rule 144A) private placements of at least $200

Table 3.1
Industry Groups Accounting For 5 Or More Sample Announcements

# of Announcements	Industry Group
70	Industrial Equipment & Machinery
62	Transportation Equipment
35	Electronics & Electronic Equipment
21	Communications
16	Chemicals & Related Products
14	Business Services
11	Air Transportation
9	Petroleum & Coal Products
9	Instruments & Related Products
9	Retail General Merchandise Stores
6	Oil & Gas Production
6	Food & Related Products
6	Railroad Transportation
6	Electric, Gas, & Sanitary Services
5	Printing & Publishing
5	Primary Metal Industries

million, and the filing dates for all medium term note programs and shelf registrations of at least $500 million.

As a rough attempt to achieve uniform coverage across issue types, the cutoff point is higher for medium term note programs and shelf registrations since individual drawdowns (for which issue-specific data were unavailable) are typically only a fraction of the total amount filed. The minimum cutoff point of $200 million was selected with the intention of ensuring that smaller offerings would not warrant the own firm productivity declines engendered by strategic preannouncements.[25] While it is true that lower levels of capital market activity might be sufficient to induce a firm to preannounce a small layoff, it is unlikely that small layoffs would have a material effect on the credit rating of the announcing firm or its rivals.

In order to determine the market's response to layoff announcements classified as strategic and non-strategic, we estimated abnormal returns around the event date for announcing firms and equal-weighted portfolios of their largest industry rivals. For the announcing firms, the abnormal return is calculated as the residual from a market model estimated using the period from 250 days before the event to 50 days before the event. The abnormal returns for a given rival portfolio consist of the residuals from a market model regression estimated using that portfolio's return from 250 days before the event to 50 days before the event. This procedure is employed to account for the cross-sectional dependence of returns realized by firms in the same industry. The market portfolio used in calculating betas for announcing firms and rival portfolios is the CRSP value-weighted portfolio. Hypothesis tests concerning the significance of abnormal returns on different days are conducted using Z statistics. The use of Z statistics gives greater weight to abnormal returns that are measured with more precision and therefore eliminates heteroskedasticity among the abnormal returns of different firms.[26]

Announcement Classification

The process of classifying the 330 sample layoff announcements as strategic or non-strategic based on observable characteristics presupposes the existence of a separating equilibrium. Managers must consider bluffing layoffs in order to influence the interest rate on borrowed funds too costly in terms of anticipated productivity losses. Also, managers must strategically preannounce only when doing so is perceived to be profitable.

The first condition, incentive compatibility, enables the capital markets to infer accurately that a layoff preannouncement signals impending layoffs. If firms with no intention of laying people off could profit by bluffing layoffs then the capital markets would have no basis for incorporating layoff preannouncements in the credit rating process. A pooling equilibrium seems unlikely in this case, however, as existing studies have found that worker fear and anxiety persist until the stated layoff targets have been achieved.[27] The prospect of instilling one's work force with unremitting anxiety should be sufficient to ensure that the incentive compatibility constraint is satisfied.

Further evidence on the costliness of bluffing comes from an analysis of announced versus actual layoffs in the dataset used by Caves and Krepps (1993). The average announced layoff in their sample of 513 Wall Street Journal layoff announcements involved 2,134 workers; however, the average actual reduction in force (measured as the change in firm employment from the beginning to the end of the calendar year in which the announcement occurred) was 4,041 workers. Although a great deal of noise surrounds the difference between announced and actual reductions in force, the finding suggests at the least that layoff announcements do not systematically overstate intended layoff targets. Results on H5 presented in Section 3.5, which indicate that strategic announcements are not more likely than non-strategic announcements to overstate intended layoff targets, also suggest that canceling announced layoffs after borrowing is not prevalent.

The second necessary condition, individual rationality, requires that firms strategically preannounce only when it is profitable to do so. Since the true motives for the timing of layoff announcements are rarely, if ever, directly observable, the most one can do is identify circumstances in which preannouncement is consistent with profit maximization. Due to the obvious difficulty of parameterizing managers' perceptions about the costs and benefits of preannouncement, we take two approaches to the classification of announcements as strategic or non-strategic.

The first approach is simply to assume that announcements immediately preceding borrowing by the firm or its rivals are strategic. This assumption is probably more tenable for bite-the-bullet cases than for bad news cases since large layoffs that are non-strategic would be unlikely to occur in firms that are simultaneously borrowing large sums of money. Therefore a number of additional requirements (described below) are imposed in order for an announcement to be classified as bad news. The second announcement classification approach involves outlining the components of the individual rationality constraint and attempting to parameterize the manager's cost-benefit tradeoff. Although the second approach is theoretically superior, the parameterization of perceptions is clearly arbitrary. Therefore, we have relegated the description of the components of the rationality constraints and their parameterization to Appendix 3.1. To simplify exposition, empirical results are reported in Section 3.5 only for the simpler classification scheme based on contemporaneous announcement and borrowing dates. Results using different parameters in the individual rationality constraint (robustness checks are described in the Appendix 3.1) are not materially different from those presented in Section 3.5 and are available upon request from the author. In any event, the results themselves suggest that announcements categorized as bite-the-bullet, bad news, and non-strategic have very distinct characteristics that argue against misclassification.

Since the bad news constraint is more difficult to satisfy than the bite-the-bullet constraint (because the announcing firm's gains are mediated by its product market interactions with its rival), we have imposed several requirements that must be met in order for an announcement to be classified as bad news.

First, the rival debt issue which follows the layoff announcement must exceed $1 billion compared to $200 million for the bite-the-bullet case. The higher borrowing hurdle ensures that rival debt offers will be very high profile industry events. Rivals are defined as the three to five largest firms (depending on the availability of CRSP data) with the same primary four digit SIC code as the announcing firm. Rival capital market activity is recorded if it is announced less than three months before the layoff announcement or is consummated within three months following the layoff announcement. Debt offerings announced by the rivals immediately prior to the layoff announcement are recorded in order to deal with the potential censoring problem that arises if the news revealed in the layoff announcement is sufficiently bad that the rival cancels the proposed debt offering altogether.[28]

The second condition requires that the announcing firm be one of the five largest (defined in terms of sales) in its principal industry. This requirement is imposed for two reasons. First, the behavior of an industry's leading firms is more likely to serve as a barometer of future industry conditions than the behavior of minor players.[29] It is important that the announcement be deemed an accurate forecast of future industry conditions because the bad news case is predicated on the correlation of firm types within an industry. Second, restricting announcing firms to be among the largest in their industries is an attempt to ensure that announcers and rivals (also constrained to be among the industry's largest firms) compete in the same strategic group and therefore confront the same external shocks. We, like Porter (1979), acknowledge the difficulty of becoming sufficiently well informed about a large sample of industries to identify their strategic group configurations, and rely on a firm's relative size within its industry as a proxy for strategic group membership.[30]

Finally, the announcing firm and its rival must compete in an industry that is sufficiently concentrated for them to recognize their strategic interdependence. The cutoff used here is a four firm concentration ratio of at least 40%. Figures in the neighborhood of 40% have been identified in a number of cross-sectional empirical studies as the point at which the concentration-profits relationship shifts discontinuously.[31]

In summary, layoff announcements are classified as bite-the-bullet if the announcing firm borrows at least $200 million and the basic individual rationality constraint is satisfied. Announcements are classified as bad news if the rival borrows at least $1 billion, the announcing firm and its capital constrained rival are industry leaders, the industry's four firm concentration ratio exceeds 40%, and the individual rationality constraint is satisfied. The remainder of the announcements were classified as non-strategic. Of the 330 sample announcements, 31 were classified as bite-the-bullet, 14 as bad news, and 292 as non-strategic. The total exceeds 330 because 7 announcements met the criteria for both strategic categories.

3.5. EMPIRICAL EVIDENCE

H1: Results on Strategic vs. Non-Strategic Lead times

In order to determine the importance of strategic information considerations in decisions about layoff announcement timing, it is necessary to analyze how announcements classified as strategic differ from those classified as non-strategic. Table 3.2 on the following page presents the mean values of several attributes germane to the strategic layoffs theory for non-strategic, bite-the-bullet, and bad news announcements.

Most interesting is the fact that the average lead time between announcement and implementation was only 3.7 months for non-strategic announcements, compared to 16.3 for bite-the-bullet and 13.3 for bad news. The extremely large differences between the strategic and non-strategic means are both statistically significant at the 5% confidence level.[32] In fact, the underlying distributions from which the samples of strategic and non-strategic announcement lead times are drawn are ordered by first-order stochastic dominance (in this case, their cumulative density functions do not overlap at all).[33] As Figure 3.2 shows, for any lead time, the fraction of non-strategic announcements exhibiting shorter lead times exceeds the fraction of strategic announcements exhibiting shorter lead times. Table 3.2 and Figure 3.2 are both supportive of H1 and suggest that informational considerations may play an important role in announcement timing decisions.

The next row presents the average size of the Wall Street Journal article reporting the layoff announcement, measured in column inches, for the three subsamples. More space appears to be devoted to strategic announcements than to non-strategic ones. Column space may be related to the degree of effort expended by the company to publicize its impending layoffs since company press releases are one of the two primary sources for Wall Street Journal articles.[34] This disparity may, however, simply reflect the fact that bigger absolute reductions in force generate more reader interest. As the next row shows, both types of strategic announcements involve much larger absolute reductions in force than do non-strategic announcements.

Since large layoffs that are non-strategic would be unlikely to occur systematically in firms that are borrowing large sums of money at the same time, the finding that strategic layoffs tend to be much larger than non-strategic layoffs seems prima facie to support the strategic layoffs theory. Small work force reductions arguably have little effect on the capital costs of the firm or its rivals. A problem with this simple interpretation is that another, perhaps more intuitively compelling, explanation exists. It could certainly be argued that the longer lead times associated with strategic layoffs are simply a function of adjustment

Table 3.2
Variable Means for Non-Strategic, Bite-the-Bullet, and Bad News Announcements

Variable	Non-Strategic Mean N = 292	Bite-The-Bullet Mean N = 31	Bad News Mean N = 14
Implementation	3.7	16.3*	13.3*
Horizon	(.39)	(3.26)	(4.38)
Article Length	6.1	8.0	8.8
	(.35)	(1.36)	(2.83)
Number of Employees	1391	6960	8508
To Be Laid Off	(160)	(2485)	(5251)
Total Employment	84,741	227,360*	294,625*
	(8449)	(40,671)	(74,125)

Standard errors are shown in parentheses.
* Indicates significantly different from Non-Strategic mean at 5% confidence level.

Figure 3.2
Distribution of Layoff Lead Times by Announcement Type

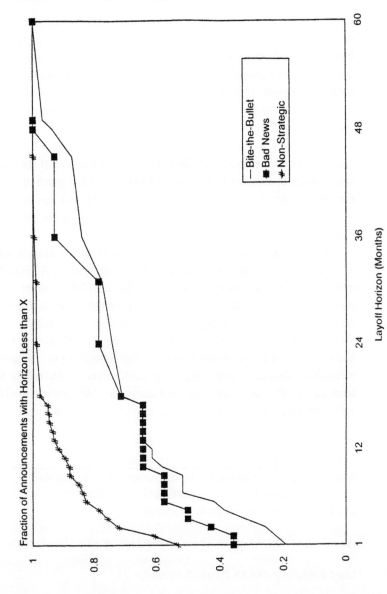

costs which are convex with respect to time. Since strategic layoffs involve, on average, five to six times as many workers as non-strategic layoffs, the reductions in adjustment costs associated with longer time lead times may more than offset the productivity losses engendered by preannouncement. It is therefore necessary to determine whether the strategic dummies are merely proxying for adjustment costs related to layoff size.

In order to investigate this possibility, we specified a TOBIT model in which the layoff lead time (LEAD) is a function of the absolute number of workers to be laid off (ABSOLAY), a quadratic term for the number of workers to be laid off (ABSQR), and dummy variables which capture the presence or absence of strategic incentives to preannounce.[36]

As Table 3.3 shows, lead times do appear to vary positively with the number of workers to be laid off. The coefficient on ABSOLAY implies that, ceteris paribus, laying off an additional 1000 workers adds roughly one month to the lead time of a representative announcement. ABSQR, although only marginally significant, suggests that the lead time is a positive, decreasing function of the number of workers to be laid off over the entire sample range.[37] After controlling for the aforementioned adjustment cost factors, the coefficients of interest for the strategic layoffs theory, those of the dummy variables, are still statistically significant and economically important.[38] The coefficient of 4.4

Table 3.3
TOBIT Analysis of Implementation Horizons

Horizon = 2.81 + .001 * ABSOLAY- .000000009*ABSQR + 4.4 * Bad News			
(.57) (.001)	(.000000005)	(1.5)	
Log Likelihood = -896.39, Pseudo R-Squared = .27			

Horizon = 2.54 + .0009 * ABSOLAY - .000000006*ABSQR + 8.9 * Bite-the-Bullet			
(.54) (.0001)	(.000000004)	(.98)	
Log Likelihood = -906.85, Pseudo R-Squared = .21			

Standard errors are shown in parentheses. Sample Size = 330.

on the bad news dummy represents the average difference in lead times between bad news and non-strategic announcements when the other regressors are held constant at their sample means. Thus, of the 9.6 month difference in average lead times for non-strategic versus bad news announcements (see Table 3.2), only 5.2 months are directly attributable to the size of the layoff. Based on a similar interpretation of the bite-the-bullet dummy coefficient, of the 12.6 month difference between non-strategic and bite-the-bullet announcements (see Table 3.2), only 3.7 months are directly attributable to layoff size.

We experimented with a number of alternative regressors to those reported in Table 3.3 in an attempt to verify that the difference in mean lead times was not attributable to omitted variable bias.[39] None of the alternative regressors proved significant. We also calculated for each sample firm the correlation between the average number of debt issues per year and the average lead time for that firm's layoff announcements (the 330 sample announcements emanate from only 181 firms). The correlation turned out to be positive but statistically insignificant. This diagnostic indicates that the subset of firms that borrowed during the sample period is not over-represented by firms which, for whatever reason, announce layoffs with long lead times. Although the inclusion of firm dummies in the TOBIT equation is infeasible, it should also be noted that of the firms which undertook multiple layoff announcements, only 4 out of 19 took longer to implement layoffs classified as non-strategic than layoffs classified as strategic. Thus, it is unlikely that the size and significance of the strategic dummy coefficients in Table 3.3 are due to unobserved firm heterogeneity.

H2 and H3: Results on Stock Price Reactions to Strategic Layoff Preannouncements

Given that the predictions about longer lead times for strategic layoffs have received empirical support, We turn now to the hypotheses regarding expected stock price reactions to strategic layoff announcements. In order to isolate the stock market's response to the sample announcements and thereby define the appropriate event window, we calculated market model excess returns for the announcing firms for each of the 11 days surrounding the layoff announcement. As Table 3.4 shows, the average return on each of the 11 days is statistically insignificant. This result is not particularly surprising given that the different situations of individual companies should elicit widely varying market reactions to layoff announcements.

We therefore performed a variance shift test on the average return for each of the 11 days in order to define the event period. Following Rohrbach and Chandra (1989), a variance shift is deemed to have occurred if the sum of standardized residuals across sample firms for a given day around the announcement date exceeds the analogously-constructed sum for at least 95% of the days during the market model estimation period. One of the virtues of this methodology is that it incorporates an empirical reference distribution of the sum of standardized residuals, thus eliminating any potential inference problems due to cross-sectional correlation. Table 3.4 reports that the p-values for each of the three days beginning one day prior to the announcement permit

Table 3.4
Evidence on the Stock Market Response to Layoff Announcements

Event Day	Mean Abnormal Return (%)	Mikkelson & Partch Z-stat.	Mean Squared Standardized Residual	Rohrbach and Chandra p-value
-5	-0.49	-0.11	0.89	0.39
-4	-0.16	-0.03	1.25	0.07
-3	-0.15	-0.03	0.86	0.47
-2	-0.13	-0.03	0.82	0.61
-1	-1.1	-0.24	1.56*	0.02
0	-1.1	-0.23	2.01**	0.01
1	0.59	0.13	1.54*	0.02
2	-0.04	-0.01	1.1	0.16
3	-0.34	-0.07	1.07	0.17
4	-0.34	-0.07	1.1	0.16
5	-0.86	-0.18	1.34	*0.05

*,** indicate significance at the 5% and 1% levels in a one-tailed p-test. Sample Size = 513. Sources for derivation of test statistics are Mikkelson and Partch (1985) and Rohrbach and Chandra (1989).

rejection of the null hypothesis of no variance shift. We therefore employ this three day event window in the analysis that follows.

It should be noted that the theory developed in this paper predicts only that bad news announcements will be considered bad news by the rivals' shareholders and bite-the-bullet announcements will be considered good news by the announcing firm's shareholders. The theory says nothing about the magnitude of stock price reactions in strategic versus non-strategic cases—we have reported the event period returns for non-strategic announcements in Table 3.5 for the sake of completeness. Further, the theory is silent on why the market responds the way it does to different types of announcements. As Caves and Krepps (1993) showed using a larger but overlapping dataset, different announcements adduce widely varying stock price reactions because they embody very different attributes.[40] Whatever the specific attributes involved, the theory developed herein asserts only that the market will view the aggregate cash flow implications as positive or negative depending on the strategic situation.

The first row of Table 3.5 shown above, which indicates that rivals suffer an average stock price decline of 1.6% for the 3 day window around bad news announcements, is consistent with the existence of

Table 3.5
Average 3 Day Excess Returns for Strategic and Non-Strategic Announcements

ANNOUNCEMENT TYPE	FIRM RETURN	PORTFOLIO RETURN
Bad News	-0.3	-1.6*
N = 14	(.025)	(.008)
Bite-the-Bullet	0.8	0.1
N = 31	(.009)	(.008)
Non-Strategic	-0.9	0.6
N = 292	(.007)	(.004)

Standard errors are shown in parentheses.
* Indicates significance at 5% confidence level.

signaling behavior in bad news cases. This decline is significantly different from zero at the 5% confidence level. Also, the percentage of rival portfolios experiencing negative returns during the event period (79%) was significantly greater than the null value of 50% at the 5% confidence level based on the Wilcoxen signed-ranks statistic.[41]

The second row of Table 3.5 shows that announcing firms experience an average stock price increase of .8% for bite-the-bullet announcements over the 3 day window. Although the average excess return around bite-the-bullet announcements is positive, the mean is indistinguishable from zero at conventional significance levels. One possible explanation for the statistical insignificance is that the cash flow implications of the announcements are masked by the stock market's anticipation of the underlying events.

H4: Results on Anticipation of Bite-the-Bullet Announcements

As noted in Section 3.1, unless the market is aware of a firm's excess employment, there is no reason for a firm to reveal its nonoptimality before borrowing. This awareness on the part of the market could temper the event period response to the point of insignificance. There are two ways to test this possibility.

First, If the stock market's expectations about the benefits of a layoff engender partial anticipation of its occurrence, then the returns to the firm should be negative during non-announcement periods.[42] We therefore calculated the estimation period returns to firms that made bite-the-bullet announcements and subtracted the estimation period returns of their rival portfolios. The average estimation period return relative to the rival portfolio was -6.4% and was significant at the 90% confidence level.[43] This piece of evidence seems to support the assertion that the market knew about the firm's excess employment and was waiting for something to be done about it.

The second method of measuring anticipation involves estimating a binary state prediction model. Utilizing a LOGIT specification, We generated predictions of the probability that a firm will announce a layoff in a given year based on publicly available data (explained subsequently) for a sample of firms that announced layoffs and a control sample that did not.[44] The dependent variable is intended to capture the market's perception of the severity of the firm's excess employment problem.[45] A finding that bite-the-bullet announcements have significantly higher predicted layoff probabilities than the non-strategic subsample could help explain the insignificance of the event period returns to these events.

The sample of announcers used in the LOGIT estimation consists of the 513 layoff announcements analyzed by Caves and Krepps (1993). The control sample of non-announcers consists of the firm-years in which a firm from the Caves and Krepps sample or one of its five largest rivals with the same primary four digit SIC code made no announcement. There were 934 instances of non-announcement for which data on the regressors was available.

On the right hand side of the LOGIT equation, operating profit as a percentage of sales (PROFIT) and cash flow (CFLOW), both lagged one year, as well as a dummy variable representing whether the firm's credit rating had been downgraded during the previous year (DWNGRADE) were included to capture the severity of employment nonoptimality and managers' ability to delay action.

Firm stock returns lagged one year (STOCKRET) were included because they are a forward-looking predictor of operating profits,[46] and because the human resource managers We surveyed indicated stock price decline as the most important layoff trigger.

Five year compound growth rates of sales (GRSALES) and number of employees (GREMP), both lagged one year, were included to account for the possibility that corporate fat accumulates rapidly during high-growth periods.[47]

A dummy variable indicating whether the firm announced a layoff during the sample period prior to the observation year (REPEAT) was added to account for the possibility that the market considers layoffs more likely if a firm's managers have previously demonstrated their willingness to fire workers.[48]

Two variables were included to control for the possibility that wealth transfers from workers to firms may motivate layoffs and therefore affect layoff anticipation. The first variable consists of unvested pension liabilities divided by the market value of the firm

(UNVESTED). This variable is set equal to zero for voluntary and temporary layoffs. The rationale behind the inclusion of this variable is that if the firm fires workers who have yet to become vested, the terminated workers' pensions revert to the firm.[49] The second consists of the difference between projected pension obligations and accumulated obligations scaled by the market value of the firm (TRAJECTORY). Some scholars have argued that this difference, based on projected wage increases for the firm's work force and the degree to which pension benefits are backloaded, may create an incentive to terminate workers.[50]

Finally, forty 2-digit SIC dummies were added to the equation to control for unobservable industry effects which might impact layoff anticipation.[51]

As Table 3.6 shows, the factors which significantly affect the estimated probability of a layoff are low profits, credit rating downgrades, poor stock price performance, and prior announcements by the same company. The equation's explanatory power (Pseudo-$R2=.24$) is rather good for this class of prediction model. More importantly, the mean predicted layoff probability for bite-the-bullet announcements (.62) is significantly higher than the mean predicted layoff probability for non-strategic announcements (.50) at the 5% confidence level. This finding, coupled with the results on returns during non-announcement periods, suggests that the insignificance of event period returns around bite-the-bullet announcements may indeed be an artifact of the market's anticipation of these events.

H5: Results on the Incidence of Bluffing

The final hypothesis concerns the incidence of strategic bluffing through the use of layoff preannouncements. The core premise on which the theory in this paper is built is that preannouncements are costly signals, not cheap talk. We therefore do not expect bluffing to occur. H5 posits that the difference between announced and actual work force reductions should be unrelated to the presence of strategic considerations. As a crude test of this assertion, we constructed a continuous variable, called BLUFF, which measures the difference between the announced work force reduction and the reduction actually realized at the end of the announced implementation period[52]. The difference in the mean values of BLUFF between the strategic and non-strategic subsamples is not remotely significant. This finding, coupled with the fact reported in Section 3.4 that the average layoff announcement does not significantly overstate the average work force reduction, provides some evidence that bluffing is not prevalent.

Table 3.6
LOGIT Estimation of Layoff Anticipation

Dichotomous Dependent Variable Represents Whether Firm X Announced a Layoff in Year Y	
Independent Variables	
PROFIT	-1.47**
	(0.40)
CFLOW	1.00E-04
	(.003)
DWNGRADE	0.84**
	(.20)
STOCKRET	-0.009**
	(.002)
GRSALES	0.49
	(.56)
GREMP	0.06
	(.74)
REPEAT	2.1**
	(.16)
UNVESTED	-0.22
	(.45)
TRAJECTORY	-0.77
	(.41)
CONSTANT	-1.24
	(.21)
+ 40 2-DIGIT SIC DUMMIES	

Log Likelihood = 51.25. Sample Size = 1447. Pseudo R^2 = .24.
Standard errors are shown in parentheses.
** Indicates significance at 1% confidence level in a two-tailed test.

3.6. CONCLUSIONS AND SUGGESTIONS FOR FUTURE RESEARCH

The theory developed in this paper and the evidence presented strongly suggest that the need to obtain outside financing—by a firm or its product market rivals—is an important determinant of costly layoff preannouncements. The principal result is that layoff announcements that immediately precede borrowing by the announcing firm or its rivals have significantly longer lead times than announcements that do not precede capital market activity. Further, the stock market responses to layoff announcements that precede borrowing are consistent with information asymmetries between managers and the capital markets that are supportive of costly yet profitable disclosure given managers' inability to contractually commit to headcount reductions.

Although most of the previous work on the interaction between product markets and capital markets suggests that capital market commitments affect product market outcomes, this paper suggests that the causal linkage between these markets is bi-directional.[53] In a classic book on managerial motivation, Donaldson and Lorsch attributed their finding that senior executives place a high value on financial self-sufficiency to managers' fear that, " . . . just when the company's vital financial and competitive interests are at stake, the market's terms [for funds] may be wholly unacceptable." [54] This paper raises the interesting possibility that the market's terms are not exogenous, but are rather a function of the strategic behavior of product market rivals.

Given the evidence that capital market activity influences a particular aspect of product market behavior, namely layoff preannouncements, the natural question for future research is whether firms use other forms of behavior as signaling devices vis-a-vis the capital markets. For example, it was recently reported in the Wall Street Journal that Chrysler was the subject of a buyout bid which would have forced the acquirers to take on more than $10 billion in debt.[55] A few days later, General Motors announced a major expansion of the Saturn program in the United States.[56] Whatever the explanation for the coincidence in timing, strategic information releases designed to influence borrowing terms for product market rivals deserve more attention.

APPENDIX 3.1

INDIVIDUAL RATIONALITY PARAMETERIZATION

As delineated in Section 3.4 of the paper, the manager's decision whether to preannounce a layoff in order to lower the firm's own borrowing cost takes the form:

$ of productivity loss due to preannouncement < $ of reduced interest cost

The productivity loss is modeled as follows:

COST=[Announced Reduction-.5*Firm Employment*.05*Announced Lead Time/12]* [.125 * (30,000 + 20,000 * White-Collar Dummy) / 12] * [(Announced Lead Time - Estimated Lead Time) / 2]

The first term represents the effective magnitude of the layoff. The size of the announced reduction, net of expected attrition over the announcement horizon (5% per year based on estimates from the Displaced Workers Survey), is included based on the premise that productivity declines are related to the probability of involuntary discharge.[57] It is assumed that productivity losses associated with the proportion of the announced reduction that is expected to occur via attrition are only half as large. If attrition is 5% per year and managers announce that the work force must shrink by 5% in the coming year, this should not cause people undue alarm over the prospect of involuntary discharge. Downsizing by means of attrition is still assumed to be somewhat costly because workers arguably suffer disutility as a result of organizational transition and turmoil.

The second term is intended to capture the dollar value of the productivity shortfall per worker per month due to preannouncement. Operationally, this shortfall is represented as one wasted hour per eight hour day multiplied by the average wage (which depends on whether the downsizing involves white-collar or blue-collar workers). The multiplier in the cost equation is the number of workers to be laid off; however, one could also conceptualize the productivity loss as applying to the entire work force with a smaller impairment factor.

The third term measures the preannouncement period potentially attributable to strategic motivation. Regression results reported in Table 3.4 suggest that, for a given lead time, the adjustment costs associated with downsizing are increasing with respect to the size of the reduction. Therefore, one can think of the fitted values from a regression of implementation lead time on adjustment cost factors as the natural duration of a downsizing. The excess duration due to strategic concerns is calculated as the announced lead time less these fitted values.[58] It is further assumed that in order to achieve their stated layoff targets, firms discharge workers at a constant rate throughout the implementation period. This formulation accords with the assumption that managers learn the exact nature of their firm's nonoptimality over time. Assuming a constant discharge rate, the third term is derived mathematically by expressing the proportion of the announced reduction remaining to be carried out each month over the announced and estimated time horizons as arithmetic series and differencing them.[59]

Finally, the entire cost term is multiplied by .2 if the layoffs were to be accomplished by offering early retirement or other voluntary severance inducements. The rationale for reducing estimated productivity losses in these cases is two-fold. First, such promises should dramatically lower the expected disutility from being laid off for those employees who fear discharge. Second, consistent with equity theory developed by scholars of organizational behavior, the productivity of those workers who feel secure in their jobs may decline less if they feel their beleaguered colleagues are being treated fairly.[60]

It should be noted that the announced horizon appears in both the first and third terms of the cost equation, with opposite signs. Because the derivative of COST with respect to the announced horizon is positive when evaluated at every point in the sample, the individual rationality constraint is biased against finding that strategic announcements have longer lead times than non-strategic announcements. The significant differences between strategic and non-strategic lead times (see Table 3.1) are therefore particularly compelling.

On the benefit side of the rationality constraint, it is possible to get a rough idea of potential capital cost savings for my sample firms because a layoff preannouncement may be expected to engender a credit rating upgrade (or protect against a credit rating downgrade). The average sample firm was assigned an A rating on its senior debt by Standard and Poor's at the end of the year prior to the layoff announcement.[61] Data on yield spreads during the sample period indicates that the average spread between long term A rated industrial bonds and long term BBB rated industrial bonds for the sample period 1987-1991 was 47 basis points.[62] Therefore a firm considering strategic preannouncement could reasonably expect its cost of capital to fall by 50 basis points following the announcement of a significant layoff.

The sample layoff announcements are considered significant by virtue of having been reported in the Wall Street Journal. This is because the two primary sources of Wall Street Journal articles are company press releases and reporters covering a geographic region or company.[63] If an announcement receives coverage in the Journal, the company and/or the newspaper considered the event worth reporting. For simplicity, a threshold effect of layoff preannouncements on capital costs is assumed, i.e. capital costs are reduced by 50 basis points or they are unaffected. The benefit side of the equation is modeled as follows:

BENEFIT = .005 * Amount Borrowed by Announcing Firm

Robustness checks in which I inflated the cost parameters stepwise by 100% resulted in the four layoff announcements with the longest lead times being classified as non-strategic. The differences between strategic and non-strategic lead times were still significant and the other results were materially unaffected.

NOTES

1. See for example Richey (1992), McCune, Beatty, and Montagno (1988), Greco and Woodlock (1989), Cameron (1994).

2. Sources cited in footnote 1 suggest that workers who deem their future dismissal imminent may suffer declines in on-the-job productivity for any of several reasons, e.g. the distractions of searching for another job, despair, and a paucity of incentives at the manager's disposal to induce effort. Monitoring costs incurred by the firm may also rise as paying efficiency wages ceases to be a viable alternative to costly monitoring.

3. For recent examples, see Neal Templin, "GM's Ratings on Senior Debt Raised a Notch," *Wall Street Journal*, May 31, 1995, pp. A5, and "Caterpillar Receives Upgrade by Moody's on $6.6 Billion of Debt," *Wall Street Journal*, June 16, 1995, pp. C20.

4. See for example Nassberg (1986), especially Chapter 13 entitled "Controlling the Borrower: Some Very Real Pitfalls".

5. Farrell and Gibbons (1989) also cite a number of papers in the incentive design literature which exploit countervailing incentives to mitigate credibility problems.

6. For example, it was reported in a Wall Street Journal article about one of the announcements in my sample, "Shearson Lehman Hutton Inc., under pressure from American Express and from credit-rating agencies, will layoff about 2,000 of its 35,000 employees in coming weeks," *Wall Street Journal*, March 1, 1990, pp. C1.

7. One can think of cases in which the correlation between optimal employment and expected profits is negative, such as when the demand curve facing the firm is rendered less elastic, but, overall, the assumption seems reasonable.

8. See for example Caves and Porter (1979) and Porter (1980), especially Chapter 7.

9. For a conflicting view, see Rumelt (1991).

10. Throughout this paper we avoid the term 'signaling' in favor of 'disclosure' because in the separating equilibria analyzed herein, the information revealed in the signal is payoff-relevant to the capital markets but the manager's type is not. This difference should not be overemphasized, as one

could certainly imagine a set of capital market conjectures (including out-of-equilibrium beliefs) under which the manager's type would be payoff-relevant in the event no signal is observed; however, to avoid confusion, the term 'disclosure' is used.

11. In these models the rival faces a grim future because, for example, the signaling firm has low costs (see Milgrom and Roberts (1982) and Saloner (1987)) or the rival has high costs (see Harrington (1987)). The costly disclosure model presented here is most similar to Harrington's in that the firm and its rival are presumed to have correlated types.

12. See for example Dierickx and Cool (1989) and Keren and Levhari (1983). Milgrom and Roberts (1987) note that,

" . . . there do seem to be important phenomena, especially in the economics of organization, that are very hard to explain without retracting at least from the assumption that transferring information, assimilating it, calculating, and deciding can be done instantaneously and without cost." (p. 188).

13. Even in the absence of strategic considerations, the lead time may be strictly positive due to the adjustment cost convexities associated with firing workers. Conceptually, one can think of the disruption to the firm's routines as an increasing function of the number of workers discharged per unit time. See Nelson and Winter (1982) especially Chapter 5.

14. In the parlance of signaling theory, the individual rationality constraint specified above is downward binding. In other words, firms whose rivals do not intend to borrow are less likely to engage in costly disclosure. See Tirole (1993).

15. There are numerous plausible explanations that deliver different layoff execution dates for good and bad managers. For example, there may be differences across managerial types in the date at which managers learn about the firm's nonoptimality. Alternatively, bad managers may suffer disutility from performing the optimal layoff while good managers do not. Descriptions of the propensity to delay needed terminations are found in the behavioral finance literature. See for example Shefrin and Statman (1985) and Statman and Caldwell (1987).

16. The simultaneous addition of capital and reduction of labor by a single activity firm may appear to contravene the logic underlying standard production functions. This seeming contradiction can be reconciled in two ways. First, a strategic shift may require a new production technique. Second, the firm may be a multi-activity firm which is reallocating resources across its portfolio of businesses from labor-intensive to capital-intensive industries.

17. This assumption seems reasonable since the debt offerings analyzed involve hundreds of millions of dollars and are therefore likely to be a part of the firm's overall capital expenditure program which presumably has its own optimal implementation time frame. In any event, all that is required in this model is that it be more costly to postpone T_1 than to accelerate the layoff announcement.

18. The theory outlined in this paper applies equally to the raising of debt and equity capital. The trips to the capital market that occurred contemporaneously with the layoff announcements analyzed herein happen to involve debt rather than equity, so the term borrowing will be used throughout. It is interesting to note that debt claims place a lighter informational burden on buyers than do equity claims, see Gorton and Pennacchi (1990). Therefore, one might expect debt pricing to be more responsive to signaling behavior than equity pricing.

19. The model would ideally be tested on debt prices; however, stock price data is used due to unavailability of sufficient debt price data.

20. If the news revealed by the layoff preannouncement is sufficiently bad, the rival may cancel the debt offering altogether. In order to deal with this potential censoring problem, H2 is tested on layoff announcements that immediately follow rivals' announced intentions to borrow as well as layoff announcements that immediately precede rival borrowing.

21. In general, the use of public announcements as event dates in event studies presupposes that capital markets rely on (and stock prices reflect) only publicly available information. Markets exhibiting this characteristic are referred to as semi-strong form efficient.

22. See Worrell, Davidson, and Sharma (1991) and Caves and Krepps (1993).

23. Formally, the layoff announcements in this model can be distinguished from cheap talk because the firm's claim about the future state of the world (i.e. the number of impending layoffs) is payoff-relevant.

24. No significant differences in layoff magnitude or market reaction were found between the included and excluded announcements.

25. Ideally, one would condition the cutoff point on layoff size; however, given the difficulty of specifying a defensible variable cutoff point, my attempt to do so has been relegated to the appendix. The empirical results are not materially different from the fixed cutoff case.

26. For a particularly clear description of the methodology used in calculating Z statistics, see Mikkelson and Partch (1985).

27. See, for example, Cameron (1994) and Greco and Woodlock (1989).

28. This control is particularly important given the statements by investment bankers on the cancellation of road shows following the release of bad news by other firms in the industry.

29. Gilbert and Lieberman (1987).

30. Porter (1979) demonstrated that the profits of firms in different size classes are determined by different factors.

31. See for example, Krepps (1997), Bradburd and Over (1982).

32. Tests of statistical significance are two-tailed tests unless otherwise noted.

33. For a formal definition, see McFadden (1989).

34. The other primary source consists of reporters covering a specific geographic region or company. See Abowd, Milkovich, and Hannon (1990).

35. It should be noted that firm employment was unrelated to implementation horizon when included as a regressor in the TOBIT equations reported in Table 4.3.

36. An econometric advantage of the announcement classification scheme based on contemporaneous announcement and borrowing dates is that simultaneity between the strategic dummies (which are a function of the implementation horizon in the parameterized individual rationality constraint) and the implementation horizon (which is a function of the strategic dummies as outlined in the TOBIT model in Table 3.3) is broken. The proximity of the borrowing date to the layoff announcement effectively serves as an exogenous instrument for the strategic dummies since it should be otherwise uncorrelated with the lead time.

37. The maxima for the two equations are achieved for layoffs of 55,000 and 75,000 workers, respectively.

38. When the strategic dummies are entered into a single equation together, the magnitude of the BAD NEWS coefficient shrinks to 1.9. This is not surprising given that 7 of the 14 bad news announcements are also classified as bite-the-bullet announcements. The single equation specification cannot be expected to capture the full impact of rival borrowing on layoff horizons because rival borrowing should not increase the implementation horizon if the announcing firm is already borrowing itself.

39. The alternative regressors included total firm employment, recent firm growth rates, industry concentration, and a dummy indicating whether the layoff was part of an overall restructuring effort.

40. Announcement attributes which turned out to be important in their study include whether white collar workers were involved, the proportion of

the firm's work force involved, the announcement of a restructuring, and the use of voluntary attrition as a means of downsizing.

41. Daniel (1978).

42. Malatesta and Thompson (1985) exploit this linkage in hypothesis tests about partially anticipated events.

43. This is not equivalent to finding that the average estimated alpha from the market models of bite-the-bullet announcers is significantly negative. The estimation period return measured here nets out the returns to other members of the announcer's strategic group, not the market return. Otherwise predicted event period returns would be positive in spite of layoff anticipation.

44. PROBIT estimation was not performed as it is theoretically inferior to LOGIT when the data are heavily concentrated in the tails of the distribution as was the case here. See Kmenta (1986).

45. Robbins and Pearce (1992) analyze the relationship between degree of retrenchment and subsequent performance, moderated by the severity of the firm's decline. They do not, however, analyze directly the relationship between severity of firm decline and degree of retrenchment.

46. It is uncertain whether stock prices are a predictor of operating profit under existing policies or under expected policies. The sign of STOCKRET should give some indication.

47. See Jensen (1993) for a detailed statement of this view. Growth of employment relative to sales was also tried, but was insignificant.

48. Blackwell, Marr, and Spivey (1990) found that significant negative returns were induced by a firm's first announcement of a plant closing (in their data base) but not by subsequent announcements.

49. For a discussion of this variable in the context of an implicit contract story, see Krepps (1995).

50. Petersen (1992) and Cornwell, Dorsey, and Mehrzad (1991).

51. In dummy variable models of sales changes, profit rates, and stock price changes, Clarke (1989) found no significant loss in explanatory power in going from three-digit to two-digit SIC dummies.

52. More precisely, BLUFF measures the difference between the announced reduction and the reduction which occurs from the year end prior to the announcement to the year end closest to the end of the announced implementation period.

53. Examples of previous work include Chevalier (1995), Bolton and Scharfstein (1990), and Maksimovic (1988).

54. Donaldson and Lorsch (1983) at 51-52.

55. See Gabriella Stern, Steven Lipin, and Pauline Yoshihashi, "Chrysler; Motives are Unclear," *Wall Street Journal*, April 13, 1995, pp. A1.

56. See Gabriella Stern, "Saturn Experiment is Deemed Successful Enough to Expand," *Wall Street Journal*, April 18, 1995, pp. B1.

57. The average displacement rate for the years 1985-1989 was 6.4%. See Bureau of Labor Statistics (1991, table 3, p. 4).

58. The following TOBIT equation was used to generate estimated horizons:

59. For example, if the announced horizon is 4 months and the estimated horizon is 2 months, excess duration is 1 month. $(1 + 3/4 + 2/4 + 1/4) - (1 + 1/2) = 1$.

60. See, for example Adams (1965) and Brockner (1988).

61. Source: Compustat. The median firm was assigned an A rating. The sample mean was 8.4 on a scale where an A rating corresponds to a value of 8 and an A- corresponds to a value of 9.

62. Salomon Brothers (1993).

63. Abowd, Milkovich, and Hannon (1990).

IV

Technological and Organizational Factors in Productivity and the Plant Closure Decision: Evidence from the Blast Furnace Industry

4.1 INTRODUCTION

The linkages between plant efficiency and plant closure have long interested economists.[1] This chapter addresses these linkages by examining a particular industry at a particular point in time: the blast furnace industry during the Great Depression. The Great Depression provides an interesting laboratory for the study of industrial evolution because of the large downturn in demand that affected the U.S. manufacturing economy quite broadly. The Great Depression has been intensely studied by macroeconomists at the aggregate level. More recently, researchers have begun to realize that the demand shocks of the Great Depression provide a unique opportunity to study how the supply side of the manufacturing economy interacted with the demand shock to produce the behavior that shows up in official statistics.[2] In the steel industry, the severe constriction of demand was one of the forces that began to mold the industry into the structure that it assumed during the 1950s and 1960s: large, integrated plants that contained all of the processes that go into producing finished steel products on single site, including blast furnaces, steel production mills, and finishing and specialty product plants.

Simple models of industry dynamics predict a "survival of the fittest" pattern of plant exit: the most inefficient plants exit first and the most efficient ones survive, thus minimizing industry-wide average cost. This class of models has implications of countercyclical productivity, that is industries are more productive during downturns because demand can be satisfied with the most efficient plants in the industry. More complex models have taken firm effects into account.[3]

Neither of these models completely describe the plant closure decisions of blast furnace plants during the Great Depression. Substantial heterogeneity in blast furnace plants existed in the early part of the twentieth century, with older plants coexisting with newer, more efficient plants built to serve the growing demand for steel. This technological heterogeneity had consequences for subsequent plant closure behavior during the Depression, when 40% of producing establishments were idle.

Two forces influenced plant closure during the period 1929–1935. First, investment in new equipment was concentrated in bigger and more efficient furnaces, so fewer furnaces were required to produce the same quantity of output. After the 1920s, marginal plants, especially those owned by non-integrated "merchant" producers, were abandoned. Second, the pattern of plant closure was influenced by the large downturn in demand for durable goods during the Great Depression. Production of steel ingots declined 57%, from 54.7 million tons in 1929 to 23.2 million tons in 1933. Plants that were technologically obsolete, due to small scale, location, or organizational structure, were shaken out during the decline in demand and stayed closed permanently. Other establishments reopened after the war-time upswing in steel demand when there was substantial investment in new plants.

This chapter analyzes productivity and plant closing patterns in blast furnace product establishments using data from the Census of Manufacturers (COM) to explore hypotheses about patterns of inefficiency, including the effects of differences in technology and differences in organizational structure. A production frontier framework is used as the basis for defining efficient performance. The production frontier is used to characterize a set of factors that are important in explaining production of iron from a cross section of plants as well as providing a metric for measuring inefficiency as the distance from the frontier. The analysis reveals some evidence that efficiency influenced plant closings; plants that closed permanently were more inefficient than plants that stayed open or closed temporarily; however, there was no significant difference in efficiency between plants that were idle for a portion of the downturn and plants that stayed open, suggesting that efficiency alone does not explain the pattern of plant closure.

Section 4.2 describes the technology of the blast furnace industry and provides the stylized facts that motivated this investigation. Section 4.3 discusses the framework for the measurement of inefficiency, including the stochastic production frontier literature and Section 4.4 describes the COM data set and specification of the production function. Section 4.5 presents the results of estimation and alternative measures of plant-level inefficiency in blast furnace plants at the beginning of the Great Depression, and Section 4.6 concludes.

4.2 STYLIZED FACTS ABOUT THE DEPRESSION-ERA BLAST FURNACE INDUSTRY

The blast furnace industry is largely a component of the integrated steel industry, the first step of the process of converting iron ore into finished steel. Blast furnaces produce pig iron, a homogenous commodity that is used primarily in its molten state as an input into basic steel production. [4]

The technology for converting iron ore into pure iron had remained basically unchanged since about 1880.[5] However, two trends affected the stock of plants and the structure of the industry. First, larger capacity furnaces became technologically feasible, and new plants incorporated the latest technology to take advantage of scale economies. Second, integrated mills that produced iron and steel at the same location provided for more efficient production because pig iron could be used in its molten form, eliminating the need to reheat it. Additional operational constraints influence the open/close decisions of a particular plant: the production of both pig iron and steel are continuous processes, with large shutdown and start-up costs. Blast furnace plants are usually operated 24 hours per day, seven days per week with the typical amount of time that a furnace runs continuously lasting six months to two years. About every four hours, molten iron is tapped out, transported either in molten form to a nearby steel mill, or cast into molds and sold. If a plant is shut down, it requires several days (as well as potentially large costs related to relining the furnace) to restart. Thus, in contrast with assembly-line type operations, adjustments to output can be achieved in increments approximately equal to furnace capacity. [6]

Because the capital stock (e.g., furnaces) in the blast furnace industry is long-lived, plants of varying ages coexisted in the 1920s and 1930s. Economic theory predicts that in long-run equilibrium, heterogeneity in production technique will not exist if certain choices are lower cost than others; however, in the short- to medium-run, it may still be worthwhile to operate rather than replace older capital, leading to a variety of technologies in operation at any point in time.

In this industry, newer plants built to serve increased demand for steel operated concurrently with older plants, generating substantial diversity in plant characteristics in 1929. Plant capacities tended to increase as newer plants were built because of larger capacities of individual furnaces as well as more furnaces per plant. These trends occurred to take advantage of scale economies that were available from larger furnaces as well as to accommodate the demand from integrated steel works for delivery of iron in bigger batches. The oldest furnace in the COM sample was built in 1845 and the newest was built in 1929, with the average vintage being pre-1900. Plants built in 1900 had hearth diameters (an indication of capacity) of 13 to 15 feet. By 1935, diameters of over 30 feet proved practical and efficient. Hearth diameters in the 1929 sample ranged from 10.5 feet to 29 feet. Clearly, the plants operating in the 1930s exhibited significant technological heterogeneity.

Firms in this industry also displayed variety in organizational form,[7] with integrated plants producing the majority of the pig iron. Merchant furnaces played an important part in the industry's early development, which is evident in the composition of plants in 1929: although merchant plants account for a small percentage of output

Table 4.1
Blast Furnace Products
Industry Aggregates

Year	Number of Establish- ments	Number of Furnaces	Production of Pig Iron (million tons)	Capacity (million tons)
1899	223	414	15.2	
1909	208	468	28.5	
1919	209	453	34.3	55.2
1929	105	316	47.4	57.3
1931	80	288	20.5	59.0
1933	72	279	14.8	56.5
1935	72	268	23.5	57.1
1939	81	236	35.3	56.3
1947	86	233	49.2	65.7

Source: Gold, Tables 17-1 and 17-2, from the COM and AISI *Annual Statistical Report*

(14%), they are still a significant fraction of the establishments (41%), and even a larger percentage of furnaces. By the 1920s, they were disappearing, as integrated steel works proved to be more efficient for the production of steel since molten iron was sent directly from blast furnace to steel work, eliminating the cost of reheating the iron.

Despite stability in the basic technology, blast furnace plant productivity increased dramatically in the early twentieth century. By 1930, the average plant produced six times as much as the average plant in 1899 and 2.5 times as much as in 1919. The use of larger furnaces, higher hot blast temperatures, mechanization of input and output handling, and to a lesser extent, improved quality of input materials, improved productivity.[8] The number of blast furnaces approximately halved from 1899 to 1947, while annual production more than tripled because of increased productivity. Table 4.1 summarizes these long run trends in production and capacity.

The structure of the COM data set allows us to examine the decisions of plant managers over time. Plant closure decisions are summarized in Table 4.2 on the following page. The COM manuscripts provide a detailed look at plant operations in any year, and because the Censuses of 1929, 1931, 1933, and 1935 are all available, a panel data set that follows plants over time has been created.[9] A plant is counted as closed in any year if there is not record of production from that plant in that year. Not surprisingly, no new plants entered into this industry during the years 1929–1935.[10] Also not surprisingly, there was substantial closure of existing plants coinciding with downturn in demand after 1929. A closer examination of the plant closures reveals some interesting patterns. In 1929, 28 of the 104 total plants closed, while 76 continued to operate in 1931; however, not all of these plants exited permanently. In fact, five of the plants that closed in 1929 reopened by 1935, and by 1945, another seven were operating again.[11] Plants closed in lesser numbers in both 1933 (11 plants not producing) and in 1933 (4 plants not producing). Only about half of the plants closed in 1929 were producing again in 1945, while most plants that closed in 1931 and 1933 were subsequently reopened. This pattern suggests that marginal plants closed first and subsequently stayed shut, while plants that closed in later years were more likely to reopen. A testable hypothesis emerges that the pattern of plant closures can be explained by plant productivity.

4.3 A FRAMEWORK FOR THE MEASUREMENT OF INEFFICIENCY

This section provides a brief discussion of alternative measures of inefficiency. Inefficiency is measured as the residual between estimated and actual output, where a production function relationship is used to determine estimated output. For a given plant, we observe actual inputs x_0 and outputs y_0. A plant is *technically* inefficient if $y_0 < f(x_0)$, where

Table 4.2
Blast Furnace Products Plant Exit, 1929–1935

	1929	1931	1933	1935
All open plants	103	75	66	68
As a subset of open plants				
Continuing	75	64	62	—
Closing	28	11	4	—
As a subset of exiting plants				
Reopen in 1933	2	—	—	—
Reopen in 1935	3	3	—	—
Reopen by 1945	7	5	3	—
Close permanently	16	3	1	—

Definitions:

All open plants: All plants that filed a COM form in a given year.

Continuing plants: Plants that are open in the next Census.

Closing plants: Plants that are closed for the next Census, either temporarily or permanently.

Source: COM manuscripts

$f(x_0)$ is the potential realization of output with inputs x_0. An inefficient plant produces less output than is possible with the inputs, given the relation between inputs and outputs. The failure to minimize costs is also a source of inefficiency; production is *allocatively* inefficient if the wrong quantities of inputs are purchased (i.e. $f_i(x_0)/f_j(x_0) \neq w_i/w_j$). The production function framework alone is useful only for getting a measure of technical inefficiency.

The textbook definition of a production function is the *maximum* output that can be produced from given inputs:

$$y = Af(x)$$

where y is output, A is an average level of productivity, and x is a vector of inputs. Estimating a production function as single equation assumes that firms buy inputs at given prices to maximize profits. There are several approaches to estimating comparative efficiency between plants within a given industry. The simplest approach estimates average productivity:

$$y = Af(x)e^v, \quad or$$
$$\ln y = \ln A + \ln(f(x)) + v \tag{1}$$

where v is an error term that allows for random disturbances. Equation (1) can easily be estimated with cross-sectional data, after choosing a functional form for f(.).[12] The term A measures the average efficiency of the industry, and the residual $y_i - Af(x_i)$ is the deviation around average productivity for an individual plant. This deviation contains both random error as well as unmeasured "inefficiency." With this framework, the effects cannot be separated.

An alternative approach uses information about plants over time. A plant-specific constant, A_i, can be estimated when the same plants appear more than once. This plant-specific constant can control for systematic differences across plants. A plant with a larger A_i is more productive. With the assumption that inefficiency is not changing over time, A_i provides a measure of plant-specific efficiency. In many cases, however, it may not be possible to estimate this intercept, either because plants are not observed over time or because the assumption that the parameter is constant does not hold.

Another strategy is to parameterize A as a function of observables that vary by plant:

$$y = A(z)f(x)e^v \tag{2}$$

where z includes observable proxies for production capabilities that are not captured in the X's. This, of course, reduces measurement error relative to estimation in equation (1). As an example, one variable that might be omitted is vintage effects of the capital stock. Because of adjustment costs, capital is optimally replaced at some interval. By including measurable differences such as vintage in the production function, systematic components that affect production can be identified, and thus excluded from the residual "inefficiency."

An alternative to measuring efficiency around an average is to compute a stochastic production frontier.[13] This relation specifies *maximum* output by making an assumption about the unobserved distribution of inefficiency, creating an envelope for the range of observations. Points are observed on or below the frontier with the distance of a firm's observed production from the frontier as a measure of its inefficiency. The stochastic production frontier uses a parametric representation of the technology and a two-part error term. A symmetric part of the error term permits random variation between plants and captures exogenous shocks. The other part of the error term represents inefficiency and is assumed to be one-sided. A variety of distributions have been used in the literature to describe the one-sided error, although the most common distributional assumption is the half-normal. The two errors are assumed to be uncorrelated. With distributional assumptions on the error term, the frontier can be estimated using maximum likelihood methods (Maddala 1983, pp. 194–196). The assumptions adopted here are that the error terms are normal and half normal, respectively. Summarizing,

$$y = Af(x)e^{\varepsilon} \qquad (3)$$

$$\varepsilon = v - u, \quad u \geq 0$$

$$v \sim N(0, \sigma_v^2)$$

$$u \sim |N(0, \sigma_u^2)|$$

$$\sigma^2 = \sigma_v^2 + \sigma_u^2$$

Here, v is a random error and u is the one-sided error that represents inefficiency. The condition $u \geq 0$ ensures that observations are generally under the frontier.[14] Output will occasionally drift above the theoretical maximum if a plant is an outlier in the tail of the random component.

This methodology yields estimates of the stochastic frontier and the parameter λ, a summary of technical inefficiency at the industry level. λ is the ratio of the variance of the asymmetric error component to the symmetric error component (σ_u / σ_v).[15] This is a straightforward summary statistic because as λ goes to zero, inefficiency becomes small or random noise becomes very large. With the distributional assumptions as maintained hypotheses, the hypothesis that inefficiency is unimportant for the entire industry can be tested by restricting $\lambda = 0$. When λ is large and significant, we can be less confident that the variables included in the production function capture the extent of underlying heterogeneity.

A plant-level measure of inefficiency allows testing of hypotheses for individual production units. The ratio of observed production to maximum production as measured by production on the frontier, where the plant operates with no inefficiency, is one such measure. So, plant-level inefficiency can be measured as

$$IE_i = 1 - \frac{E(Y_i | X_i, u_i)}{E(Y_i | X_i, u_i = 0)}$$

This measure is easy to interpret. The value of IE_i ranges between zero and one; for a given plant, if $u_i = 0$, IE_i would equal zero, indicating no inefficiency. Unfortunately, u_i is unobserved, so IE cannot be calculated directly; however, ε_i (the observed two-part error term) and the parameters λ and σ^2 contain information about the realization of u_i, and the literature suggests a method for estimating the conditional expectation $\hat{E}(u_i | \varepsilon_i)$ as a proxy for plant-level inefficiency.[16]

4.4 COM DATA AND SPECIFICATION OF A PLANT-LEVEL PRODUCTION FUNCTION

Since the Census and industry sources provide a rich set of data on inputs and technology but little information on the value or costs of capital, a production function relation will be used to measure technical inefficiency. Although the Census does contain longitudinal information for some plants, it is not well suited for studying long-run differences in inefficiency because of the dramatic changes in the number of plants and in capacity utilization that occurred during the Great Depression. After 1929, many of the most inefficient plants closed and drop out of the sample, creating substantially less variance in technical efficiency across establishments. Those units that did remain open after 1929 operated at less than full capacity, confounding the measurement of short-run and long-run inefficiency.

For these reasons, technical efficiency is measured by estimating a production function from the 1929 cross-section of plants with some of the observable, systematic differences across plants controlled for by including various components of the capital stock in the production function estimates. The use of a peak year minimizes difficulties of interpreting efficiencies of establishments that are operating below full capacity. Presumably with the contraction of demand in the early 1930s, plants used only the most efficient units, making the capital stock a poor approximation of the capital input that was actually utilized. This fact was dramatically true in 1933, when capacity utilization was 33%. Since technological variables are altered slowly, they are taken as exogenous in consideration of the 1929 cross-section.

The statistical calculations of productivity are based on a unique and valuable data source, the Census of Manufacturers' manuscripts for blast furnace products establishments.[17] The Census surveys all establishments with production over $5,000, providing data on output quantity and value, employment, cost of materials, and capital stock. The capital stock data provided by the Census is not ideal since the Depression-era Census did not include questions about the value of capital. In 1929 and 1935, the survey included a question about the horsepower of the capital stock, and this can be used as proxy for mechanization. The Census also recorded the number of furnaces in the plant. Table 4.3 presents industry-wide means for Census variables.

Because the COM manuscripts have detailed plant name, owner-ship, and location, the Census data was supplemented with additional information about technology and organization at the plant level. From the American Institute of Iron and Steel (AISI) directories, data on technological characteristics including vintage of furnaces, hearth size of furnaces, and overall annual plant capacity were added. Organizational structure was proxied with a dummy variable for merchant status; a plant is classified as a merchant blast furnace if its parent firm had no steel making capacity.

The remainder of this section develops a set of observable variables that measure production capabilities and allow for heterogeneity across plants. The Census provides good information on iron production and wage earners employed. Output (TON) is measured as tons of iron produced. It is not a bad approximation to call pig iron homogenous. An alternative measure of output (WTTON) weights tons of higher-valued specialty iron by its relative price. Labor input is wage earner months (WEM). WEM is the sum of wage earners employed in each month, a good approximation of labor input since plants operate 24 hours a day with employment typically adjusting through the number of workers rather than through hours per worker.

Measuring the capital stock is less straightforward, since the Census itself provides only crude measures. If all furnaces were identical, then using the number of furnaces in a plant would be a useful measure of the capital stock. More furnaces would imply greater capacity, and hence more output; however, the number of furnaces alone is an inadequate measure since furnaces varied in attributes and plants differed in auxiliary equipment utilized. The crude measure of the number of furnaces (FURN) is supplemented with additional characteristics related to furnace productivity. Total hearth size (TOTHS) is the sum of the diameters of all of the furnaces in the plant. A furnace with a larger hearth size was more productive, since energy and labor could be utilized more efficiently. Once hearth size is controlled for, the coefficient on furnaces is expected to be negative, implying that it was more

Table 4.3
Blast Furnace Products
Establishment Means[a]

	1929	1931	1933	1935
Value of products[b]	7,442 (8,574)	4,130 (3,722)	3,186 (2,971)	5,482 (5,115)
Cost of materials[b]	5,889 (6,847)	3,264 (2,939)	2,756 (2,554)	4,405 (3,976)
Steel production[c]	410 (472)	244 (215)	200 (179)	310 (284)
Wage earner months	2,899 (2,640)	2,132 (1,627)	2,111 (1,683)	2,626 (1,801)
Wages[b]	406 (384)	252 (202)	170 (143)	273 (226)
Salaried Employees	23 (24)	na	16 (17)	21 (23)
Salaries[b]	66 (65)	na	34 (34)	54 (55)
Number of Establish-ments	103	75	66	68

a: Computed over usable sample. Standard errors in parentheses.

b: In thousands of dollars.

c: In thousands of tons.

Source: COM Manuscripts

productive to have a single large furnace than two smaller furnaces of
the identical capacity. Vintage is measured in two ways: the vintage of
the newest furnace (NVINT) and average vintage of all furnaces
(VINT). It is assumed that newer capital is correlated with lower-cost
production, since newer furnaces could incorporate the latest technological changes. However, anecdotal evidence suggests that when furnaces were periodically rebuilt, it was possible for them to be expanded, therefore making it possible for older furnaces to enjoy improved scale economies (Hogan 1950). Horsepower (HP) measures
total horsepower, and proxies for mechanization. Plants with more
horsepower presumably operated more auxiliary equipment (i.e., machinery for handling inputs and outputs). In fact, most of the cost of
building a blast furnace came from installation of blowing engines and
associated equipment, so installed horsepower is indicative of "real"
capital stock (Allen 1977 p. 610). This set of variables will be used
together to measure capital.

Both an "average practice" production function, using ordinary
least squares, and a "best practice" production function, using a stochastic production frontier, will be estimated. Cobb-Douglas is the
functional   form   for   the   production   functions:
$Y = c + \alpha L + \beta K + \varepsilon$, where Y is the log of output, L is the log of
labor, and K is the log of capital. Although the Cobb-Douglas form is
somewhat restrictive, more flexible functional forms yield the same
general conclusions. Descriptive statistics for variables used in the regressions are listed in Table 4.4. The estimating sample excludes one
plant that did not report the horsepower variable, leaving 103 observations.

4.5 RESULTS OF ESTIMATION AND ALTERNATIVE
MEASUREMENTS OF INEFFICIENCY

In order to examine technological and organizational contributions to
productivity and to analyze plant-level inefficiency, several variations
of both average and best-practice production functions are estimated.

Table 4.4
Descriptive Statistics

TON	tons of steel, 1929
WTTON	tons of basic steel + 3.7* tons of specialty steel
WEM	wage earner months
FURN	number of furnaces
DYPC	total days operated/365
HP	horsepower of motors + prime movers
TOTHS	sum of the diameter of all hearths
MERCHANT	= 1 if firm has no steel making capacity

Number of observations: 103

	MEAN	STD DEV	MINIMUM	MAXIMUM
TON	409965.27	472133.48	1038.00	2714982.00
WTTON	423733.75	475404.48	3840.60	2714982.00
WEM	2899.41	2640.92	101.00	14410.00
FURN	2.65	2.27	1.00	12.00
DYPC	0.93	0.17	0.085	1.00
HP	26324.57	40720.88	25.00	303817.00
TOTHS	57.99	56.03	10.50	301.15
MERCHANT	0.42	0.50	0.00	1.00

Standard errors in parentheses.

The results are summarized in Table 4.5. In addition to specifications that include crude measures of capital and labor, estimated equations contain observable sources of plant heterogeneity, including variation in capital stock and organizational structure. This section tests hypotheses of the effects of these variables on plant-level productivity, and then goes on to examine the correlation of inefficiency and the plant open/shut decision.

The first specifications include the roughest (and most traditional) measures of productive inputs. In columns (1) and (2) of Table 4.5, labor input is measured as the log of wage-earner months and capital input is measured as the log of the number of furnaces in a plant, a measure of capital that constrains variation in the capital stock across plants to one narrowly defined measure of capital, the number of furnaces. The first column is the standard OLS estimation of the production function, while the second column approximates best practice by estimating a stochastic production frontier using maximum likelihood methods. Comparing (1) and (2), we notice several things. First, the coefficient on the constant term increases, indicating the production frontier has shifted out from average practice, an intuitively sensible result. Second, the coefficient on capital, or its output elasticity, increases for plants operating at the frontier, suggesting that more efficient plants operated with less labor and more capital.[18] Third, comparisons of average and best practice suggest that plants in this industry operate below the frontier. The hypothesis that technical inefficiency is unimportant for the industry as a whole can be tested by comparing the maximum likelihood estimates to the OLS estimates. The likelihood ratio test statistic is 11.4, highly significant for $X^2_{(2)}$, suggesting that the hypothesis that blast furnaces in 1929 were technically efficient can be rejected.

To control for plant-level differences in capital stock, including the scale and age of furnaces as well as the extent of overall mechanization of material handling, several other specifications were analyzed. Specifications (3) and (4) add TOTHS and HP, to control for heterogeneity in the capital stock in the plant. As a group, the inclusion of TOTHS and HP variables greatly improves the explanatory power of the regression, suggesting that the observable differences in plants are

Table 4.5
Production Function Estimates

	(1)	(2)	(3)	(4)
Dependent Variable:	LTON	LTON	LTON	LTON
Estimation Method:	OLS	ML	OLS	ML
C	3.624	7.221	-0.038	2.721
	(0.944)	(0.930)	(1.324)	(1.168)
LWEM	1.102	0.716	0.576	0.282
	(0.136)	(0.130)	(0.132)	(0.130)
LFURN	0.354	0.532	-1.829	-1.686
	(0.166)	(0.176)	(0.523)	(0.384)
LHP			0.147	0.131
			(0.064)	(0.048)
LTOTHS			2.124	2.145
			(0.501	(0.309)
MERCHANT				
R^2	0.754		0.852	
σ^{-1}		0.977		1.307
λ		4.256		4.548
		(2.049)		(2.406)
LL	-99.23	-93.53	-74.13	-61.81
n	103	103	103	103

Standard errors in parentheses.

Table 4.5 (*continued*)
Production Function Estimates

	(5)	(6)	(7)	(8)
Dependent Variable:	LTON	LTON	LWTON	LWTON
Estimation Method:	OLS	ML	OLS	ML
C	1.187	3.482	2.519	3.922
	(1.339)	(1.433)	(1.197)	(1.367)
LWEM	0.631	0.378	0.453	0.325
	(0.128)	(0.127)	(0.115)	(0.115)
LFURN	-1.499	-1.382	-1.352	-1.201
	(0.516)	(0.466)	(0.461)	(0.495)
LHP	0.149	0.140	0.125	0.127
	(.061)	(0.048)	(0.055)	(.050)
LTOTHS	1.655	1.69	1.702	1.658
	(0.480)	(0.483)	(0.454)	(0.498)
MERCHANT	-0.382	-0.312	-0.227	-0.148
	(0.128)	(0.183)	(0.115)	(0.170)
R^2	0.864		.869	
σ^{-1}		1.374		1.68
λ		4.29		1.963
		(1.860)		(0.653)
LL	-69.64	-57.59	-59.10	-55.07
n	103	103	103	103

important in characterizing production.[19]   Alternative specifications (not reported here) explore the effect of the age capital. Vintage effects were found to be insignificant, suggesting that mechanization and hearth size describe the differences across plants more clearly than the initial age of the furnace. Consistent with the first pair of regressions, the output elasticity of labor decreases between average- and best-practice plants. Although the sum of variances is decreasing (σ^{-1} is increasing) from column (2) to column (4), the coefficient on λ remains large. Therefore, the addition of capital stock characteristics does not account for the source of differences in efficiency and distance from the frontier; average inefficiency is not reduced to zero. In fact, the variation in average inefficiency is not reduced by better measurement of capital, suggesting that while technological factors better explain the variance in output, much of the inefficiency must flow from organizational or other roots.

Another possible source of inefficiency could be the consequence of organizational form. This effect could be purely organizational or explainable by differences in technology. Merchant plants tended to be smaller, and may have had less-skilled managers. This would imply a negative coefficient on a MERCHANT dummy. Alternatively, merchant plants may have utilized inputs in different proportions than integrated plants, possibly having less-mechanized input handling and more complex output processing. The second explanation would imply that merchant plants had a different production process than their integrated counterparts, that could be measured as a production function with slope shifts across merchant and integrated producers.

Columns (5) and (6) investigate these hypotheses about organizational form and productivity. The variable MERCHANT, equaling one if the plant was not affiliated with a steel works, is added to the regressions. The coefficients on labor and capital are consistent with prior specifications. The MERCHANT coefficient enters into the regression significantly negatively, providing some support for differences across organizational forms, although the magnitude of this effect is not large compared with constant term. To test whether this difference is purely organizational or has roots in different production technology, the slopes of inputs are allowed to vary across plants. The restriction of common slopes cannot be rejected at the 5% level. (The regressions are not reported here.)[20] The organizational characteristic seems to be proxying for some difference between merchant and integrated producers that is not technological, providing weak support for organizational differences in productivity.

To incorporate the variety in composition of output, a new dependent variable that weights output of specialty iron by its relative price is constructed. Specialty iron sold for about $70 per ton in 1929 versus $19 per ton for basic pig iron. Although this output was a very small percentage of total output, some smaller plants produced only specialty iron. This specification is reported in columns (7) and (8). This change decreases the magnitude of λ, suggesting that the composition of output explains some of the variance in the one-sided error. The coefficients compared to equations (5) and (6) do not change much, but λ, the unexplained variance, drops from 4.3 to 1.8. This result suggests that the large average inefficiency was being driven by a few outliers that were not well-characterized by the set of technology proxies. It is also worth noting that in the enhanced specification, major change in coefficients between the average and best practice estimations is in the constant term. The coefficients are fairly stable between columns (7) and (8), especially compared with the big shifts that we observed between columns (1) and (2). This suggests that the finding of more intensive use of capital at best practice plants is evidence of a misspecification of the production function.

The estimates in Table 4.5 are used to calculate technical inefficiency at individual plants. For each plant, $1 - \hat{E}$ $(e^{-u_i}|\varepsilon_i)$, the expected value of the inefficiency part of the two-sided error term conditional on the residual, is estimated to summarize the distance from the frontier at each plant.[21] The distribution of the distance from the frontier is summarized in Table 4.6, which lists the frequencies of plants in various ranges, using the production functions in columns (6) and (8). Not surprisingly, the two measures are highly correlated. The most inefficient plants tended to be small plants outside of the main locus of steel production.

Table 4.6
Summary of Plant-Level Inefficiency Measures

	(1)	(2)
	Output	Adjusted Output
Percent Inefficiency	Number of Plants	Number of Plant
0–10%	3	2
10–20%	17	17
20–30%	27	46
30–40%	21	19
40–50%	16	9
50–60%	8	5
>60%	11	5

Note: Column (1) is calculated using specification (6) and column (2) is calculated from specification (8) of Table 4.5.

How are plant inefficiency and plant closure related? Given the stylized facts discussed in Section 4.2, one might expect that plants that closed were more inefficient than plants that remained open. Examining plant inefficiency conditional on whether a plant was open, idle, or closed over the sample period reveals some interesting patterns. Plants that stayed open all four Census years, on average, were significantly more efficient than plants that closed permanently in this time period.[22] Plants that idle were more efficient than plants that closed permanently, although this difference is only marginally statistically significant (at the 90% significance level). Interestingly, there was no difference in efficiency between plants that are temporarily closed and those that are open all four years of the sample. This evidence suggests that inefficient firms were indeed permanently driven out by the large downturn in demand, but that forces beyond static efficiency were influencing the pattern of plant closure that observed during the Great Depression.

Many blast furnace plants are part of a larger integrated plant that is fixed in geographic and product space. Although these characteristics are out of the realm of the blast furnace plant narrowly defined, the demand for products of the associated steel mill is a very important factor on the operations of plants over the 1929–1935 period.[23] Because of the nature of the production process (continuous with real efficiency gains from coordination) more than just the productivity of the blast furnace plants affect the plant open/shut decision. In this industry, the integrated nature of the firm drives decisions that might, on their face, appear to violate cost minimization.

4.6 CONCLUSIONS

This chapter employs frontier production models to examine "best practice" technology in Depression-era blast furnace plants and examines estimates of inefficiency derived from estimates of the frontier. Since inefficiency is measured as a residual, good proxies for the heterogeneous capital stock are included to measure systematic variance in the data that would otherwise be lumped in that residual inefficiency measure. This approach makes sense in an intra-industry study when there is substantial information about variety of technology. The 1929 COM, supplemented with industry sources, provides rich data to study plant-level output in the blast furnace industry.

Several conclusions can be drawn from the analysis of the 1929 cross-section of blast furnace plants. First, the difference between the production technology of an average and the most efficient plants is much less pronounced as we improve the measurement of inputs and outputs. Perhaps earlier results finding more capital intensive technology at best practice plants reflect a misspecification of the production relation, rather than a real difference in technology. Second, inclusion of a group of capital proxies explains much of the variance in output. These proxies represent significant heterogeneity that is present in the capital stock. On average, however, the unobserved inefficiency is still important. Third, there is weak support for differences in productivity across organizational structure, once technology and product mix has been controlled for. The coefficient on the dummy for merchant plants is negative and significant, although small in magnitude. These differences are not explained by different production processes at integrated and merchant facilities.

Finally, an examination of estimates of plant-level efficiency suggests that less efficient plants closed permanently during the large downturn in demand. However, the closing of plants that were idle during part of the 1929–1935 period but later reopened when demand rebounded cannot be explained by efficiency alone, since efficiency measures for these "mothballed" plants look similar for plants that remained open during the Depression. Other strategic factors must be influencing firm decisions on temporary closure.

NOTES

1. See Baily, Hulten, and Campbell (1992) for an investigation of productivity and industry dynamics using the data from modern Censuses of Manufacturing.

2. Margo (1993) provides an overview of labor research, Bresnahan and Raff (1991) examine dynamics in the auto industry, and Bernanke and Parkinson (1991) look at the labor market in the interwar economy using industry-level data.

3. See e.g., Ghemawat and Nalebuff (1990) for a theoretical model and Deily (1988) for an empirical analysis of plant investment and closure decisions in the modern steel industry.

4. There is some variation in the chemical composition of pig iron, but as a first approximation, the product is homogenous. Ferro-alloys, an expensive specialty iron, accounted for about 1% of total tonnage in 1929. Although this was not important as percentage of industry output, eight smaller plants produced primarily specialty iron.

5. See Temin (1964) and Hogan (1971) for an early history of the industry. For a more complete description of the technology, see Alderfer and Michl (1950) or Camp and Francis (1925).

6. This is a slight oversimplification with the introduction of fanning in the 1930s, a technique that allowed furnaces to operate at lower throughput rates. See Haven and Buell (1933).

7. Merchant plants produce and sell pig iron. Non-integrated firms purchase steel and produce finished goods. Semi-integrated plants fabricate steel and produce finished shapes. Integrated steel plants perform all of these functions. (Alderfer and Michl 1950)

8. Gold, et al. (1984), pp. 471–484 provide a catalog of incremental technological improvements to furnaces 1900–1970.

9. Bresnahan and Raff (1990) and Bertin (1994) describe the construction and contents of the database.

10. No new entry in this time period is supported by Hogan (1971), p. 1133.

11. Operation after 1935 was tracked using later editions the American Institute of Iron and Steel directory. The presence of a listing in a later directory, often corroborated by evidence of recent maintenance work, indicated that a plant was only temporarily closed.

12. See Griliches and Ringstad (1971) for an application.

13. See Aigner et al. (1977) for an early article about implementation of this technique. Schmidt (1985–1986) and Bauer (1990) provide thorough reviews of the literature, and Caves and Barton (1990) use the frontier approach to analyze productivity in U.S. manufacturing.

14. The distribution can be truncated at some point other than zero, complicating the calculations but leaving the basic framework unchanged.

15. This is not the only way to summarize this information. Lee and Tyler (1978) derive a measure of efficiency as the expected value of actual to frontier output. Their measure depends only on the standard deviation of the asymmetrical component of the residual.

16. Jondrow et al. (1982) calculate the conditional expectation

$\hat{E}(u_i | \varepsilon_i)$ as a measure of u_i. Battese and Coelli (1988) show that if the production function is in logs- the usual Cobb-Douglas assumption-then we want

to estimate $1 - \hat{E}(e^{-u_i} | \varepsilon_i)$ to measure plant-level inefficiency.

17. Although a single establishment often operated blast furnaces and steel works on the same site, the data for blast furnaces products are reported separately from steel works and rolling mills. See Bertin (1994) for a detailed description of the COM data.

18. Other ML estimates of frontier production functions have also found this. See Albach (1980), Forsund and Jansen (1977), and Lee and Tyler (1978) for comparisons of best and average practice.

19. The likelihood ratio test statistic, comparing specification (3) and (4) is 63.44, which allows us to reject the hypothesis that plant-level heterogeneity is zero.

20. Note that results are different with alternative dependent variables. If we control for differences in output (either with WTTON or a dummy for spe-

cialty producers) there is no difference in coefficients. With unweighted meas-ure of output, the coefficients are significantly different at the 99% level.

21. Since the production function used here is in logs, inefficiency is measured as

$$IE_i = 1 - \frac{e^{(x_i\beta+v_i-u_i)}}{e^{(x_i\beta+v_i)}} = 1 - e^{-u_i}$$

This expression is evaluated using the conditional expectations

$1 - \hat{E}(e^{-u_i}|\varepsilon_i)$ to obtain a value for inefficiency at the plant level. See Jondrow et al. (1982) for a more complete derivation.

22. Here are the means of inefficiency variable by operating status from column (1) of Table 4.6. The results look similar for column (2).

Status	N	Mean	Std Deviation
open (1)	60	.312	.148
idled (2)	23	.330	.198
closed (3)	20	.51	.220

We tested for significant differences in the means, using the following test statistic:

$$t = \frac{(\bar{x}_1 - \bar{x}_2)}{\sqrt{s_1^2/n_1 + s_2^2/n_2}}$$

where $\bar{x}_1$ and $\bar{x}_2$ are the sample means, s_1^2 and s_2^2 are the sample variances, and n_1 and n_2 are the sample size.

23. See Bertin, Bresnahan, and Raff (1996) for a detailed analysis of labor productivity in this industry as demand fluctuates.

Bibliography

Abowd, John M., George T. Milkovich, and John M. Hannon. "The Effects of Human Resource Management Decisions on Shareholder Value." *Industrial and Labor Relations Review* 43 (February 1990): 203-236.

Adams, J.S. "Inequity in Social Exchange." In *Advances in Experimental Social Psychology*. Volume 2. L. Berkowitz, ed. New York: Academic Press, 1965.

Aigner, Dennis J., C.A. Knox Lovell, and Peter Schmidt. "Formulation and Estimation of Stochastic Frontier Production Function Models." *Journal of Econometrics* 6, no. 1 (1977): 21-37.

Albach, Horst. "Average and Best Practice Production Functions in German Industry," *Journal of Industrial Economics* 29 (1980): 55-70.

Alchian, Arman, and Harold Demsetz. "Production, Information Costs, and Economic Organization." *American Economic Review* 62 (December 1972): 777-795.

Alderfer, E.B., and H.E. Michl. *Economics of American Industry*. New York: McGraw-Hill Book Company, Inc., 1950.

Allen, Robert. "The Peculiar Productive History of American Blast Furnaces 1840-1913." *Journal of Economic History* 37, no. 3 (1977): 606-633.

American Institute of Iron and Steel. *Annual Statistical Report*. Washington DC: AISI, various years.

American Institute of Iron and Steel. *Directory of Iron and Steel Works in the United States and Canada*. New York: AISI, 1930, 1935, 1938, 1945.

Baldwin, John R., and Richard E. Caves. "Foreign Multinational Enterprises and Merger Activity in Canada." In *Corporate Globalization through*

Mergers and Acquisitions. Edited by Leonard Waverman. Investment Canada Research Series. Calgary: University of Calgary Press, 1991.

Baily, Martin N., Charles Hulten, and David Campbell. "Productivity Dynamics in Manufacturing Plants." *Brookings Papers on Economics Activity: Microeconomics* (1992): 187-249.

Battese, George E., and Tim J. Coelli. "Prediction of Firm-Level Technical Efficiencies with a Generalized Frontier Production Function and Panel Data." *Journal of Econometrics* 38, no. 3 (1988): 387-399.

Bauer, Paul W. "Recent Developments in the Econometric Estimation of Frontiers." *Journal of Econometrics* 46, nos. 1-2 (1990): 39-56.

Berman, Eli, John Bound, and Zvi Griliches. "Changes in the Demand for Skilled Labor within U.S. Manufacturing Industries." NBER Working Paper No. 4255, 1993.

Bernanke, Ben S., and Martin L. Parkinson. "Procyclical Labor Productivity and Competing Theories of the Business Cycle: Some Evidence from Interwar U.S. Manufacturing Industries." *Journal of Political Economy* 99, no. 3 (1991): 439-59.

Berndt, Ernst R., Catherine J. Morrison, and Larry S. Rosenblum. "High-Tech Capital Formation and Labor Composition in U.S. Manufacturing Industries: An Exploratory Analysis." Working Paper No. 4010, National Bureau of Economic Research, 1992.

Bertin, Amy. "Competition and Productivity in the Depression-Era Steel Industry." Ph.D. diss., Harvard University, 1994.

Bertin, Amy, Timothy F. Bresnahan, and Daniel Raff. "Localized Competition and the Aggregation of Plant-Level Increasing Returns: Blast Furnaces, 1929-1935." *Journal of Political Economy* 104, no. 2 (1996): 241-266.

Bhagat, Sanjay, Andrei Shleifer, and Robert W. Vishny. "Hostile Takeovers in the 1980s: The Returns to Corporate Specialization." *Brookings Papers on Economic Activity: Microeconomics* (1990): 1-84.

Blackwell, David W., M. Wayne Marr, and Michael F. Spivey. "Plant-closing Decisions and the Market Value of the Firm." *Journal of Financial Economics* 26 (August 1990): 277-288.

Blair, Margaret M., ed. *The Deal Decade: What Takeovers and Leveraged Buyouts Mean for Corporate Governance.* Washington: Brookings Institution, 1993.

Blair, Margaret M., Sarah J. Lane, and Martha A. Schary. "Patterns of Corporate Restructuring, 1955-87," Brookings Institution, Working Paper No. 91-1, 1991.

Bloch, Harry. "Prices, Costs, and Profits in Canadian Manufacturing: the Influence of Tariffs and Concentration." *Canadian Journal of Economics* 7 (November 1974): 594-610.

Bolton, Patrick, and David S. Scharfstein. "A Theory of Predation Based on Agency Problems in Financial Contracting." *American Economic Review* 80 (March 1990): 93-106.

Bradburd, Ralph M. and A. Mead Over, Jr. "Organizational Costs, 'Sticky Equilibria,' and Critical Levels of Concentration." *Review of Economics and Statistics* 64, no. 1 (February 1982): 50-58.

Bresnahan, Timothy, and Daniel Raff. "The American Manufacturing Economy in the Time of the Great Depression." Unpublished manuscript, 1990.

Bresnahan, Timothy F. and Daniel Raff. "Intra-Industry Heterogeneity and the Great Depression: The American Motor Vehicles Industry, 1929-1935." *Journal of Economic History* 51 (1991): 317-331.

Brickley, James A., and Leonard D. Van Drunen. "Internal Corporate Restructuring: An Empirical Analysis." *Journal of Accounting and Economics* 12 (January 1990): 251-280.

Brockner, Joel. "The Effects of Work Layoffs on Survivors: Research, Theory, and Practice." *Research in Organizational Behavior* 10 (1988): 255.

Brynjolfsson, Erik, and Lorin Hitt. "Is Information Systems Spending Productive? New Evidence and New Results." Working Paper #3571-93, Sloan School of Management, MIT, 1993.

Cameron, Kim S. "Strategies for Successful Organizational Downsizing." *Human Resource Management* 33 (1994): 188-211.

Camp, James M., and Charles B. Francis. *The Making, Shaping, and Treating of Steel*, 4th ed. Pittsburgh: Carnegie Steel Corporation, 1925.

Caves, Richard E. "Trade Exposure and Changing Structures of U.S. Manufacturing Industries." In *International Competitiveness*, edited by A. Michael Spence and Heather A. Hazard. Cambridge, MA: Ballinger, 1988.

Caves, Richard E. *Adjustment to International Competition: Short-Run Relations of Prices, Trade Flows, and Inputs in Canadian Manufacturing Industries.* Ottawa: Economic Council of Canada, 1990.

Caves, Richard E., and Associates. *Industrial Efficiency in Six Nations.* Cambridge: The MIT Press, 1992.

Caves, Richard E., and David R. Barton. *Efficiency in U.S. Manufacturing Industries.* Cambridge: The MIT Press, 1990.

Caves, Richard E., and Matthew B. Krepps. "Fat: The Displacement of Nonproduction Workers from U.S. Manufacturing Industries." *Brookings Papers on Economic Activity Microeconomics* 2 (1994): 227-288.

Caves, Richard E., and Michael E. Porter. "From Entry Barriers to Mobility Barriers: Conjectural Decisions and Contrived Deterrence to New Competition." *Quarterly Journal of Economics* 91 (May 1977): 241-261.

Chevalier, Judith A. "Capital Structure and Product-Market Competition: Empirical Evidence from the Supermarket Industry." *American Economic Review* 85, no. 3 (June 1995): 415-435.

Clarke, Richard N. "SICs as Delineators of Economic Markets." *Journal of Business* 62, no. 1 (1989): 17-31.

Cornwell, Christopher, Stuart Dorsey, and Nasser Mehrzad. "Opportunistic Behavior by Firms in Implicit Pension Contracts." *Journal of Human Resources* 26 (1991): 704-725.

Cyert, Richard M., and James G. March. *A Behavioral Theory of the Firm.* Englewood Cliffs, NJ: Prentice-Hall, 1963.

Daniel, W. W. *Applied Nonparametric Statistics.* Boston: Houghton Mifflin, 1978.

Deily, Mary E. "Investment Activity and the Exit Decision." *The Review of Economics and Statistics* 70, no. 4 (1988): 595-602.

Delehanty, George E. *Nonproduction Workers in U.S. Manufacturing.* Amsterdam: North-Holland, 1968.

Dertouzos, Michael L., Richard K. Lester, and Robert M. Solow. *Made in America: Regaining the Competitive Edge.* Cambridge: MIT Press, 1989.

Dierickx, Ingemar and Karel Cool. "Asset Stock Accumulation and Sustainability of Competitive Advantage." *Management Science* 35, no. 12 (December 1989): 1504-1514.

Domowitz, Ian, R. Glenn Hubbard, and Bruce C. Petersen. "Business Cycles and the Relationship between Concentration and Price-Cost Margins." *Rand Journal of Economics* 17 (spring 1986): 1-17.

Donaldson, Gordon, and Jay W. Lorsch. *Decision Making at the Top.* New York: Basic Books, 1983.

Dunne, Timothy, Mark J. Roberts, and Larry Samuelson. "Patterns of Firm Entry and Exit in U.S. Manufacturing Industries." *Rand Journal of Economics* 19 (winter 1988): 495-515.

Farber, Henry S. "The Incidence and Costs of Job Loss: 1982-1991." *Brookings Papers on Economic Activity: Microeconomics* 1 (1993): 73-132.

Farrell, Joseph, and Robert Gibbons. "Cheap Talk with Two Audiences." *American Economic Review* 49, no. 5 (December 1989): 1214-1223.

Forsund, Finn, and Eileve Jansen. "On Estimating Average and Best-Practice Production Functions via Cost Functions." *International Economic Review* 18, no. 2 (1977): 463-76.

Freeman, Richard B., and James L. Medoff. "Substitution between Production Labor and Other Inputs in Unionized and Nonunionized Manufacturing." *Review of Economics and Statistics* 64 (May 1982): 220-233.

Geroski, Paul A. "Entry, Innovation and Productivity Growth." *Review of Economics and Statistics* 71 (November 1989): 572-578.

Ghemawat, Pankaj, and Barry Nalebuff. "The Devolution of Declining Industries" *The Quarterly Journal of Economics* 105, no. 1 (1990): 167-186.

Gilbert, Richard J., and Marvin Lieberman. "Investment and Coordination in Oligopolistic Industries." *RAND Journal of Economics* 18, no. 1 (spring 1987): 17-33.

Gold, Bela, et al. *Technological Progress and Industrial Leadership: The Growth of the US Steel Industry 1900-1970.* Lexington, Massachusetts: Lexington Books, 1984.

Gorton, Gary, and George Pennachi. "Financial Intermediaries and Liquidity Creation." *Journal of Finance* 45, no. 1 (March 1990): 49-71.

Greco, Philip A., and Brenda K. Woodlock. "Downsizing the Organization." *Personnel Administrator* (May 1989): 105-108.

Griliches, Zvi, and V. Ringstad. *Economies of Scale and the Form of the Production Function: An Economic Study of Norwegian Manufacturing Establishment Data.* Amsterdam: North-Holland, 1971.

Hammer, Michael, and James Champy. *Reengineering the Corporation: A Manifesto for Business Revolution.* New York: Harper Business, 1993.

Hamermesh, Daniel S. "The Demand for Labor in the Long Run." In *Handbook of Labor Economics.* Edited by Orley Ashenfelter and Richard Layard. Amsterdam: North Holland. Vol. 1, 1986: 429-471.

Harrington, Joseph E., Jr. "Oligopolistic Entry Deterrence Under Incomplete Information." *RAND Journal of Economics* 18, no. 2 (summer 1987): 211-231.

Haven, William A., and W. C. Buell, Jr. "Blast Furnace Activities in 1932." *Blast Furnace and Steel Products* 21, no. 1 (1993): 32-34.

Healy, Paul M., Krishna G. Palepu, and Richard S. Ruback. "Does Corporate Performance Improve after Mergers?" *Journal of Financial Economics* 21 (April 1992): 135-175.

Herz, Diane E. "Worker Displacement in a Period of Rapid Job Expansion, 1983-87." *Monthly Labor Review* 113 (May 1990): 21-33.

Hogan, William T. *Productivity in the Blast-Furnace and Open-Hearth Segments of the Steel Industry: 1929-1946.* New York: Fordham University Press, 1950.

Hogan, William T. *Economic History of the Iron and Steel Industry in the United States.* Volume 3. Lexington, Massachusetts: Lexington Books, 1971.

Holmstrom, Bengt R. "Moral Hazard in Teams." *Bell Journal of Economics* 13 (Autumn 1982): 324-340.

Holmstrom, Bengt R., and Jean Tirole. "The Theory of the Firm." In *Handbook of Industrial Organization.* Edited by Richard Schmalensee and Robert D. Willig. Amsterdam: North-Holland. Vol 1, 1989: 61-133.

Jensen, Michael C. "The Modern Industrial Revolution, Exit, and the Failure of Internal Control Systems." *Journal of Finance* 48, no. 3 (July 1993): 831-880.

Jondrow, James, C.A. Knox Lovell, Ivan Materov, and Peter Schmidt. "On the Estimation of Technical Inefficiency in the Stochastic Production Function Model." *Journal of Econometrics* 19, nos. 2-3, (1982): 233-238.

Katz, Lawrence F., and Kevin M. Murphy. "Changes in Relative Wages, 1963-1987: Supply and Demand Factors." *Quarterly Journal of Economics* 107 (February 1992): 35-78.

Keren, Michael, and David Levhari. "The Internal Organization of the Firm and the Shape of Average Costs." *Bell Journal of Economics* 14 (autumn 1983): 474-486.

Kmenta, Jan. *Elements of Econometrics.* New York: Macmillan, 1986.

Krepps, Matthew B. "Corporate Layoffs, Shareholder Value, and the Breach of Implicit Employee Contracts." In A. Raj Joshi and Greg Nelson, eds., *Downsizing.* Boston: Harvard Business School Press, 1995: 21-27.

Krepps, Matthew B. "Another Look at the Impact of the National Industrial Recovery Act on Cartel Formation and Maintenance Costs." *Review of Economics and Statistics* 79, no. 1 (1997): 151-154.

Lee, Lung-fei, and William Tyler. "The Stochastic Frontier Production Function and Average Efficiency: An Empirical Analysis." *Journal of Econometrics* 7, no. 3, (1978): 385-89.

Lehrer, Robert N., ed. *White Collar Productivity.* New York: McGraw-Hill, 1983.

Lichtenberg, Frank R., and Donald Siegel. "Productivity and Changes in Ownership of Manufacturing Plants." *Brookings Papers on Economic Activity* 3 (1987): 643-673.

Lichtenberg, Frank R., and Donald Siegel. "The Effect of Ownership Changes on the Employment and Wages of Central Office and Other Personnel." *Journal of Law and Economics* 33 (October 1990): 383-409.

MacDonald, James M. "Does Import Competition Force Efficient Production?" Working paper, Rensselaer Polytechnic Institute, 1992.

Maddala, G.S. *Limited and Dependent Variables in Econometrics.* Cambridge, England: Cambridge University Press, 1983.

Maksimovic, Vojislav. "Capital Structure in Repeated Oligopolies." *Rand Journal of Economics* 19, no. 3 (Autumn 1988): 389-407.

Malatesta, Paul H., and Rex Thompson. "Partially Anticipated Events." *Journal of Financial Economics* 14 (1985): 237-250.

Margo, Robert A. "Employment and Unemployment in the 1930s." *Journal of Economic Perspectives* 7, no. 2, (1993): 41-59.

McCune, Joseph T., Richard W. Beatty, and Raymond V. Montagno. "Downsizing Practices in Manufacturing Firms." *Human Resource Management* 27 (Summer 1988): 145-161.

McFadden, Daniel. "Testing for First-Order Stochastic Dominance." In Thomas B. Fomby and Tae Kun Seo, eds., *Studies in the Economics of Uncertainty in Honor of Josef Hadar*. New York: Springer-Verlag, 1989: 113-134.

Mikkelson, Wayne H., and M. Megan Partch "Stock Price Effects and Costs of Secondary Distributions." *Journal of Financial Economics* 14 (1985): 165-194.

Milgrom, Paul, and John Roberts. "Limit Pricing and Entry Under Incomplete Information: An Equilibrium Analysis." *Econometrica* 50 (1982): 443-460.

Milgrom, Paul, and John Roberts. "Informational Asymmetries, Strategic Behavior, and Industrial Organization." *American Economic Review* 77, no. 2 (May 1987): 184-193.

Murphy, Kevin M., and Finis Welch. "The Role of International Trade in Wage Differentials." In *Workers and Their Wages: Changing Patterns in the United States*. Edited by Marvin H. Kosters. Washington: AEI Press, 1991: 39-69.

Nassberg, Richard T. *The Lender's Handbook*. Philadelphia: American Law Institute, 1986.

Nelson, Richard R., and Sidney G. Winter. *An Evolutionary Theory of Economic Change*. Cambridge: Harvard University Press, 1982.

Nickell, Stephen J., Sushil Wadhwani, and Martin Wall. "Productivity Growth in UK Companies 1975-86." *European Economic Review* 36 (June 1991): 1055-1085.

Niskanen, William A., Jr. *Bureaucracy and Representative Government*. Chicago: Aldine-Atherton, 1971.

Petersen, Mitchell A. "Pension Reversions and Worker-Stockholder Wealth Transfers." *Quarterly Journal of Economics* (1992): 1033-1056.

Porter, Michael E. "The Structure Within Industries and Companies' Performance." *Review of Economics and Statistics* 61 (May 1979): 214-228.

Porter, Michael E. *Competitive Strategy: Techniques for Analyzing Industries and Competitors*. New York: The Free Press, 1980.

Pugel, Thomas A. "Foreign Trade and US Market Performance." *Journal of Industrial Economics* 29 (December 1980): 119-130.

Ravenscraft, David J., and F. M. Scherer. *Mergers, Sell-Offs, and Economic Efficiency*. Washington: Brookings Institution, 1987.

Rayner, Derek G. "A Battle Won in the War on the Paper Bureaucracy." *Harvard Business Review* 53 (January-February 1975): 8-14.

Revenga, Ana L. "Exporting Jobs: The Impact of Import Competition on Employment and Wages in U.S. Manufacturing." *Quarterly Journal of Economics* 107 (February 1992): 255-284.

Richey, Mark W. "The Impact of Corporate Downsizing on Employees." *Business Forum* (summer 1992): 9-13.

Robbins, D. Keith, and John A. Pearce II. "Turnaround: Retrenchment and Recovery." *Strategic Management Journal* 13 (1992): 287-309.

Rohrbach, Kermit, and Ramesh Chandra. "The Power of Beaver's U Against a Variance Increase in Market Model Residuals." *Journal of Accounting Research* 27, no. 1 (spring 1989): 145-155.

Rumelt, Richard. "How Much Does Industry Matter?" *Strategic Management Journal* 12 (1991): 167-185.

Salomon Brothers. *Analytical Record of Yields and Yield Spreads.* New York, Salomon Brothers, Inc., 1993.

Saloner, Garth. "Predation, Merger, and Incomplete Information." *RAND Journal of Economics* 18 (summer 1987): 165-186.

Scherer, F. M., and Kevin Huh. "R&D Reactions to High-Technology Import Competition." *The Review of Economics and Statistics* 74 (May 1992): 202-212.

Schmalensee, Richard. "Do Markets Differ Much?" *American Economic Review* 75, no. 3 (June 1985): 341-351.

Schmidt, Peter. "Frontier Production Functions." *Econometric Reviews* 4, no. 2, (1985-86): 289-328.

Shefrin, Hersh, and Meir Statman. "The Disposition to Sell Winners Too Early and Ride Losers Too Long: Theory and Evidence." *Journal of Finance* 40 (July 1986): 777-792.

Shleifer, Andrei, and Lawrence H. Summers. "Breach of Trust in Hostile Takeovers." In *Corporate Takeovers: Causes and Consequences*, edited by Alan J. Auerbach. Chicago: University of Chicago Press, 1988: 33-56.

Statman, Meir, and David Caldwell. "Applying Behavioral Finance to Capital Budgeting: Project Terminations." *Financial Management* 16, no. 4 (winter 1987): 7-15.

Statman, Meir, and James F. Sepe. "Project Termination Announcements and the Market Value of the Firm." *Financial Management* 18 (winter 1989): 74-81.

Sumanth, David J., Vincent K. Omachonu, and Mario G. Beruvides. "A Review of the State-of-the-Art Research on White-Collar/Knowledge Worker Productivity." *International Journal of Technology Management* 5, no. 3 (1990): 337-355.

Temin, Peter. *Iron and Steel in Nineteenth-Century America: An Economic Inquiry.* Cambridge, Massachusetts: MIT Press, 1964.

Tirole, Jean. *The Theory of Industrial Organization.* Cambridge, MA: MIT Press, 1993.

U.S. Bureau of Economic Analysis. *National Income and Product Accounts of the United States, 1959-88.* Washington: Government Printing Office, 1992.

U.S. Bureau of Economic Analysis. *Business Statistics, 1963-91.* Washington: Government Printing Office, 1992.

U.S. Bureau of Industrial Economics. *1983 U.S. Industrial Outlook.* Washington: U.S. Department of Commerce, 1983.

U.S. Bureau of Labor Statistics. *Displaced Workers, 1985-1989.* Bulletin No. 2382. Washington: Bureau of Labor Statistics, 1991a.

U.S. Bureau of Labor Statistics. *Employment, Hours, and Earnings, United States, 1909-90.* Bulletin No. 2370. Washington: Bureau of Labor Statistics, 1991b.

U.S. Bureau of the Census. *Fifteenth Census of United States: Manufactures 1929.* Washington, DC: United States Government Printing Office, 1929.

U.S. Bureau of the Census. *1970 Census of Population,* Subject Reports, *Occupation by Industry.* PC(2)-7C. Washington: Government Printing Office, 1972.

U.S. Bureau of the Census. *1980 Census of Population.* Vol. 2, Subject Reports, *Occupation by Industry.* PC80-2-7C. Washington: Government Printing Office, 1984.

U.S. Bureau of the Census. *The Relationship Between the 1970 and 1980 Industry and Occupation Classification Systems.* Technical Paper 59, by Paula L. Vines and John A. Priebe. Washington: Bureau of the Census, 1989.

Williamson, Oliver E. "Managerial Discretion and Business Behavior." *American Economic Review* 53 (December 1963): 1032-1057.

Worrell, Dan L., Wallace N. Davidson III, and Varinder M. Sharma. "Layoff Announcements and Stockholder Wealth." *Academy of Management Journal* 34 (September 1991): 662-678.

Wruck, Karen H. "Financial Distress, Reorganization, and Organization Efficiency." *Journal of Financial Economics* 27 (October 1990): 419-444.

Index

For Product Safety Concerns and Information please contact
our EU representative GPSR@taylorandfrancis.com or Taylor & Francis
Verlag GmbH, Kaufingerstraße 24, 80331 München, Germany

For Product Safety Concerns and Information please contact
our EU representative GPSR@taylorandfrancis.com Taylor & Francis
Verlag GmbH, Kaufingerstraße 24, 80331 München, Germany

T - #0054 - 160425 - C0 - 216/138/9 [11] - CB - 9780815330172 - Gloss Lamination